8 Questions God Can't Answer?

JOHN BUSACKER

TO ELVIN MONROE "MONTY" SHOLUND

My dear mentor:

His penetrating questions ignited my faith.

His persistent encouragement instilled God's calling.

Cover design by Garborg Design Works, Inc.,
Savage, Minnesota

Published by *Life*-Worth, LLC, Minneapolis, Minnesota

Printed in the United States of America

CONTENTS

A Word Before

THIS IS A BOOK OF QUESTIONS.

If you are looking for answers—put this book back!

I have a lot of questions, especially in these uncertain times. Where are we heading? How will this all turn out? Will we be OK? Have we hit bottom yet? What is the prudent course of action? Where is God in all of this?

Jesus had a lot of questions too. He was not just idly passing time or seeking to learn more about us with all of His inquiries. The God who cares about the location of every sparrow on the planet, and has the very hairs on our heads numbered, already knows all of our answers. There is nothing that stumps God. There is no additional knowledge that he must acquire. No hidden feeling that he must expose to himself. No wisdom that he must glean. He already knows everything about you and me.

So if God knows so much, why does he ask so many questions?

Jesus' principle teaching style was to ask questions—tough questions, personal questions, searching questions, transforming questions. He yearns to transform our faith—from feeble to fierce, from predictable to passionate.

By answering his questions for ourselves, we begin to discover the true object of our desire, the source of our fear, the uniqueness of our identity, the focus of our compassion, the real measure of our wealth, and the only lasting love of our life.

Are you willing to risk living in God's questions? The adventure will undoubtedly cause you to experience uncertainty and restlessness. But the result of leaning into Jesus' questions is the exhilaration of a faith that is untamed in its expression and unimaginable in its outcome. It is worth the wild ride!

Join me in exploring **8 Questions God Can't Answer** for us. The departure point for our journey together is the simple, yet deeply challenging question of our desire, "*What do you want?*" The destination is the pivotal question of our devotion, "*Do you truly love me?*" The path of our own faith pilgrimage is mapped out in these 8 questions.

Deepen your spiritual adventure by completing the Study Journal at the conclusion of each chapter. The Study Journal consists of three parts:

> **READ** additional scripture to expand your
> understanding of each question.

> **REFLECT** on questions to stimulate discovery
> and small group dialogue.

> **RESPOND** to a challenge to boldly practice
> each of Jesus' questions.

So, if you are looking for questions—this is the book for you!

JB

What Do You Want?

DESIRE

The next day John was there again with two of his disciples. When he saw Jesus passing by, he said, "Look, the Lamb of God!" When the two disciples heard him say this, they followed Jesus. Turning around, Jesus saw them following and asked,

"What do you want?"

John 1:35–38

What do you want?

ELIAS' CRITICAL QUESTION

I was immediately drawn to Elias. A short, powerfully built man with a radiant smile, Elias (Swahili for Elijah) had stopped counting his successful Kilimanjaro summit attempts when he had reached 200. At age 30, he already emanated the quiet wisdom of experience and the clear passion of calling that inspired confident followership. If I were going to attempt the summit of Kilimanjaro, I wanted Elias to be my guide.

My eleven fellow climbers and I gathered around in a tight circle as Elias kneeled over a dog-eared map of the mountain. He described the route through 5 eco-systems we would be taking in our ascent and descent of Kilimanjaro. We would begin in the Montane forest, camp the fourth evening in the Reusch crater bracketed by the 75-foot ice wall of the Fortwangler Glacier, summit early the next morning, then descend along the Mweka route. All told, the journey would take 6 days. Elias pointed out landmarks on the topographic map and described both the physical and emotional obstacles we would encounter during the climb. As he spoke, we were all feeling the giddy anticipation of success, the quiet fear of possible failure, and a chafing restlessness to begin—the powerful mixture that precedes most great adventures in life.

After less than 15 minutes, Elias ended his narrative, slowly turned to look each of us directly in our heart and asked, "What do you want?" Great question! What did we want? Elias used our answers to quickly build relationships from which he would encourage and challenge each of us in unique ways over the next

6 days. His ability to effectively lead us was in direct proportion to the clarity of our own desires.

JESUS' FIRST QUESTION.

Jesus asked the same question early in His ministry. It is the first crucial question he used to ignite followership in 12 men who would change the world forever with the power of his teaching. It is the essence of how he engages us today to continue his world-changing work. He continues to ask, through both subtle stirrings and traumatic life events, "What do you want?" It is the first question he cannot answer for us. We must weigh in for ourselves.

The two men whom Jesus asked the original question were followers of John the Baptist. There was a wildness about John that attracted these men and many others to the wilderness. He stood as the thunder in the desert[1] sent by God to show everyone where to look and who to believe in.[2] He had the same clear passion of calling as Elias, igniting the energy of a whole generation of people weary of Roman oppression and a worn-out religion of rules. When Jesus showed up on the scene, John pointed him out for all of his followers to see. With just one word and two days' experience, these two disciples of John abruptly turned and began to run after Jesus. What a stunning change of allegiance.

There must have been something missing from the disciples' lives, some "Holy discontent" deep within their hearts, that they sensed only this carpenter from Nazareth could satisfy.

---

1   John 1:23, Eugene H. Peterson, *The Message* (MSG)
2   John 1:6 (MSG)

Despite being avid followers of John, they dropped everything and turned on a dime to pursue a different leader. They were *seekers*, as Os Guinness describes, "looking for something. They were people to whom life, or a part of life, had suddenly become a point of wonder, a question, a problem, or a crisis. This happened so intensely that they were stirred to look for an answer beyond their present answers and to clarify their position in life."[3] Jesus' very presence was posing a new question for which they had no answer. The followers of John became seekers of Jesus.

What about you? Are you a seeker also? Do you have a sense that something deep inside is missing? Has life become a point of wonder, a question, a problem or a crisis for you? Is there a restlessness that is unstilled by work, school, friendship, money, church or even family? Do you feel as if you are treading water, making no progress? If so, perhaps God is asking you the same question today—"What do you want?"—with the intent to engage you in a new world-changing work. What do you *really* want?

WAITING FOR DESIRE TO HAPPEN

We want to maintain at least the illusion that we are all buttoned down and in control of our life, work, relationships and religion—that we are always moving steadily forward. But then God poses a new question in our heart's stirring, causing us to again become a seeker. We are awakened by a new question in our soul and consumed by finding a new answer.

Author Brennan Manning, who learned through the depths of alcoholism that control is an illusion, encourages us to pray, "I

---

3 Os Guinness, *The Call,* 4

surrender my will and my life to you today, without reservation and with humble confidence for you are my loving Father. Set me free from self-consciousness, from anxiety about yesterday and tomorrow and from the tyranny of the approval and disapproval of others, that I may find joy and delight simply and solely in pleasing you. Let your plan for my life and the lives of all your children gracefully unfold one day at a time."[4]

I regularly charge off after my own desires before checking in on God's direction. It is said that human beings are the only creatures that speed up when lost. David sums up God's perspective on speed in Psalm 130: "I pray to God—my life a prayer—and *wait* for what he'll say and do."[5] Paradoxically, the initial path of seeking is to wait. David had discovered two critical truths about godly waiting. First, he is not shooting up a prayer at the last minute in hopes of getting some personal request granted. His *life* was a prayer. Much of the Psalms are David's prayer journal with God. He was in constant, intimate, brutally honest conversation with the Almighty. Second, he was not waiting for God to catch up to his plan. We are never ahead of God. We need simply to look to where God is already active and join him there. An African expression for patience is "Waiting for time to happen." We must wait for God's desire to happen, in our heart.

What we are often searching for is the wisdom to discern God's will at each critical transition in our lives. This wisdom does not typically flow into a noisy, crowded mind. It seeps into a heart quieted by prayer. God's desire is a matter of the heart, not just the head. The word *desire* is most often coupled in the Bible with

---

4 Brennan Manning, *Ruthless Trust*, 132
5 Psalm 130:5 (MSG)

heart or *heart's desire*. Erwin McManus writes, "What can settle your mind will not settle your soul. It will stir it up."[6] The desire of the heart is a much more powerful tug than that of the head.

My friend John, a Carmelite Monk, whose life is devoted to discerning matters of the heart through constant prayer, sent me this thought several years ago: "The inner life of prayer can best flourish in an atmosphere of silence, free from agitation and noise. In silent prayer we come face-to-face with ourselves and learn to reconcile the contradictions of our lives; the fears, anxieties and frustrations that lead to discouragement and illness. Something more begins to happen, mysteriously, in moments of deep serenity; we discover at the root of our being, the presence of the One who created us and calls us in love, and we emerge from this experience transformed by the quiet joy and gentle peace which radiates from the inner recesses of the heart."

God approached Solomon centuries ago with the same question. "Ask for whatever you want me to give you."[7] In other words, *what do you want*, Solomon?

There was no salary cap on these contract negotiations, no limitations on what Solomon could ask for or on what God could grant. Signing bonus? No problem. Guaranteed contract? Money? Fame? Power? Done. What Solomon asked for was simply wisdom, a discerning heart to govern God's people and to distinguish between right and wrong.[8] God replied, "Since this is your *heart's* desire. . .wisdom and knowledge will be given you."[9] I hesitate to think what I would ask for given the open

---

6 Erwin Raphael McManus: "Soul Cravings"; *Catalyst*, November 2006
7 2 Chronicles 1:7
8 1 Kings 3:9
9 2 Chronicles 1:11,12

checkbook of heaven! And yet God's hand is open to give us our heart's desire IF (and this is the critical IF) our heart's desire is God's desire. How do we know if they are one and the same? How do we discern if the longings of our heart are God-inspired?

BLINDED BY THE WHITE

Webster's New World Dictionary defines *orientation* as "The homing faculty of certain animals."[10] We are all born with a spiritual homing faculty. Instinctively, we know if we are on or off course. St. Augustine wrote, "You have made us for Yourself, and our hearts are restless until they find their rest in You." Restlessness is our God-given homing faculty. Try as we may with work, recreation, food, sex, family, money, religion or whatever else, we often feel lost—so disoriented that only God can find us.

The advertising industry in the U.S. spends billions of dollars annually trying to jam our homing devices. They bombard us through pop-ups, e-mails, TV, radio, newspapers, magazines, billboards and phone calls with over 3,000 ads per day.

Through brilliantly crafted messages, their job is to create desire. If we look like _____, drive _____, smell like _____, wear _____, and so forth, we will be happy, successful, fulfilled. You fill in the blanks. In a word, their role is to disorient us. But to become disoriented is to risk becoming quickly lost.

I was climbing in late spring at Mt. Rainier National Park with our older son Brett. We had gotten off to a late start, but were still hoping to climb from the parking lot of Paradise (aptly

10 Webster's New World Dictionary, 1003

named) to the ranger hut at Camp Muir, an ascent of about 5,000 feet. The weather was deteriorating with intermittent periods of sun, snow, clouds, rain and gusty winds. At about the halfway point, two climbers descending from the summit met us. They cautioned us that the conditions at Camp Muir were "downright nasty" and suggested we turn around soon. Heeding their advice, Brett and I decided to hike just a hundred feet farther, enjoy the view and begin our descent back to the car.

No sooner had we turned around, when we were suddenly enveloped by a complete whiteout, a dense cloud that swallowed us both up, immediately eliminating any sense of direction or depth perception. Our eyes filled with dancing white spots as our brains tried to register our distance to any discernable mountain feature. We were both disoriented almost instantly. I had a dull fear that, although we were off the glacier and in no danger of falling into a crevasse, we might still miss our destination and spend quite some time wandering in circles. Our saving grace that afternoon was a series of brightly colored wands planted every 10–20 yards in the snow by the U.S. Park Service, outlining the path to Paradise.

It is painfully easy to become quickly disoriented in our journey through life, caught up in the whiteout of our own desires and thus in danger of wandering in circles on the path to Paradise. One minute it seems that we are navigating in the clear sunshine of God's calling and in the next we are lost in a deep cloud bank of our own causing. Our homing faculty tells us that we are off track, but we need wands to find our way out. Thankfully, God anticipated our tendency to become disoriented and planted wands to help us navigate our way home.

Paul cautioned the people of Rome to "not conform any longer to the pattern of this world, but be transformed by the renewing of your mind. Then you will be able to test and approve what God's will is—his good, pleasing and perfect will."[11]

God's words are our wands. If we are going to be able to discern between good and bad desires, we need to regularly spend time in His book sharpening our mind. God's words are "living and active,"[12] or as Eugene Peterson describes in *The Message*, "His powerful Word is sharp as a surgeon's scalpel, cutting through everything, whether doubt or defense, laying us open to listen and obey."[13] If we are to cut through the dense cloud bank of media noise in order to discern God's desire, we must follow the wands of His words. God's desires always line up with His words. He is perfectly consistent.

Listening to our heart and reading the Word can still lead us a long way off course. History is riddled with examples of ungodly acts that have been committed in the name of "God's will." Scripture is the narrative of God's great love for us. Wisely used, it lovingly displays God's desires through our actions. It does not indiscriminately endorse our point of view or merely prove our position over others.

We must, therefore, triangulate our heart's desires and our own understanding with the wisdom of other Jesus-following friends. The Bible is full of encouragement to seek the counsel of others willing to love us and speak truth to action in our life and plans. "The way of a fool seems right to him, but a wise man listens to advice."[14] "Plans fail for lack of counsel, but with many advisers

---

11 Romans 12:2
12 Hebrews 4:12
13 Hebrews 4:12 (MSG)
14 Proverbs 12:15

they succeed."[15] "Form your purpose by asking for counsel, then carry it out using all the help you can get."[16]

Without the wisdom and encouragement of others, we are prone to pursue selfish desires, or perhaps worse yet, fun desires (even good desires) but not God's desires. The enemy of great is what is merely good. There is nothing inherently wrong with good desires, except that they may keep us from pursuing God's great desires.

In a stunning observation at the recent REVEAL conference at Willow Creek Church, Bill Hybels suggested that the largest gap in faith-practice exists not between seekers and believers, but between immature followers and Jesus-centered followers. The less mature believe that God is for their plans and agenda. Jesus followers have given up their lives and plans in complete surrender to him. It is no longer about them.

This is the great and deliberate contradiction in Jesus' first question. Even though he asks what we want, he is not for *our* plans. He is for *His* plans, planted in our heart, supported by His Word and confirmed by other Jesus-followers. The essence of His question is not about *our* desire, it is about discovering *His* desire for us. In the end, what will truly quench our desires is a relentless pursuit of His desire. Nothing else will satisfy.

The insatiable outcomes of our own pursuits bear this out.

---

15 Proverbs 15:22
16 Proverbs 20:18 (MSG)

How's that working for you?

When our two sons were teenagers and we saw them charging down a path that we sensed would not have a positive outcome, we tried to sneak up on them with the powerful checking question, "How's that working for you?" This is a great question to assess the pursuit of our heartfelt desires as well. Our choices have consequences.

Imagine being a contestant on a game show where you must choose between what is behind either Door #1 or Door #2. Let me list the items behind both doors:

Door #1

- repetitive, loveless, cheap sex
- a stinking accumulation of mental and emotional garbage
- frenzied and joyless grabs for happiness
- trinket gods
- magic-show religion
- paranoid loneliness
- cutthroat competition
- all-consuming yet never-satisfied wants
- a brutal temper
- impotence to love or be loved
- divided homes and divided lives
- small-minded and lopsided pursuits
- the vicious habit of depersonalizing everyone into a rival
- uncontrolled and uncontrollable addiction
- ugly parodies of community

Door #2

- affection for others
- exuberance about life
- serenity
- willingness to stick with things
- sense of compassion in the heart
- conviction that a basic holiness permeates
  things and people
- loyal commitments
- not needing to force our way in life
- able to marshal and direct our energies wisely[17]

Which door would *you* choose? The rewards behind Door #1 or Door #2 are ours to receive as we decide daily which desires to pursue. The first door is a path of our own selfish desires, the second a path of God-inspired desires. Door #1 lives are marked by the restlessness of disorientation, always wanting more or different, never having a sense of rest from striving or freedom from worry. Door #2 lives are marked by a deep joy and contentment because the desires pursued are in tune with God's heart.

As God regularly continues to ask us, "What do you want?" we must wait and listen to our heart, weigh our desires against God's words, seek wise counsel from faithful others, and then regularly check the outcomes of our pursuits.

---

17 Galatians 5:19–23 (MSG)

BUYING TIME

What do you want? This is God's crucial first question. We are not wired as human beings created in the image of God to merely replicate, but to learn and grow, to adventure and explore. Our desire defines our direction and ultimately our destination. What we pursue reflects who we are and determines what we will become.

It is like saying, "Show me who you hang with and I'll show you who you'll become." The followers of John wanted to hang with Jesus, and ultimately became like him.

John's two disciples' response to Jesus' question was a startled, "Where are you staying?" They were not sure how to respond to such a direct inquiry. Their initial safe answer was a benign question of their own. I suspect they were buying time. Why get to the heart of the matter if they could stick to the news, weather and sports? John's disciples sensed danger in Jesus' question.

I, too, feel unsettled when God plants longings in my heart. There is the intuitive sense that I must move from my comfort zone, and in that moment lurks the realization that another great adventure is about to begin. The feelings of giddy anticipation, quiet fear and chafing restlessness return.

In *Wild at Heart*, John Eldredge writes, "Most men think they are simply here on earth to kill time—and it's killing them. But the truth is precisely the opposite. The secret longing of your heart, whether it's to build a boat and sail it, to write a symphony and play it, to plant a field and care for it—those are the things you were made to do.

But it's going to take risk, and danger, and there's the catch. *Are we willing to live with the level of risk God invites us to?* Something inside us hesitates."[18]

This is why Jesus knew he had to ask us the next question to move us forward in our faith journey, a question to get at the core of our fear: *"Why are you so afraid?"*

---

18 John Eldredge, *Wild at Heart*, 49, italics added

Chapter One

WHAT DO YOU WANT?

READ
the following Scripture:
- 2 Chronicles 1:7–12
- Galatians 5:19–23 (Preferably in *The Message*)

REFLECT
on the following questions:
1. Are you a *seeker*? What is currently stirring in your heart?
2. How do you determine if your desires are bad?
Merely good? Godly?
3. Which of the items behind Door #1 or #2 (Galatians 5:19–23)
most accurately capture the outcomes of your pursuits?

RESPOND
to the following challenge:
- Commit to spending time each of the next 30 days in God's
Word—seeking His "wands" for your life. The Old Testament
book of *Proverbs* would provide you with great daily wisdom.

-or-

- Commit to finding and engaging one or several Jesus-followers
who will give you wise counsel, ask the tough questions
and hold your toes to the coals of your commitments
in the next 30 days.

Why Are You So Afraid?

FEAR

That day when evening came, he said to his disciples, "Let us go over to the other side." Leaving the crowd behind, they took him along, just as he was, in the boat. There were also other boats with him. A furious squall came up, and the waves broke over the boat, so that it was nearly swamped. Jesus was in the stern, sleeping on a cushion. The disciples woke him and said to him, "Teacher, don't you care if we drown?" He got up, rebuked the wind and said to the waves, "Quiet! Be still!" Then the wind died down and it was completely calm. He said to his disciples,

"Why are you so afraid?"

Mark 4:35–40

Why are you so afraid?

WHAT IF?

One memorable commercial several years ago featured a woman swimming laps in a pool. Back and forth, back and forth. Suddenly she stopped, stood up and removed her goggles with a quixotic look. The silent words that appeared on the TV screen were simply, "What if?" The implication was that as she was swimming, her mind was pondering possibilities that culminated with a workout-stopping big idea. What if?

What if? What if we risk taking action on the desires God plants in our hearts? What if we practice salmon faith and swim upstream against the torrential current of the world's values and teachings? So much of what Jesus taught was directly opposite of the "wisdom" of His day. His teaching is just as revolutionary in our day as well. What if we trust His radical teaching today? What if we risk refocusing our resources on the poor and the lost? What if…what if we *really* take God seriously?

Stefan, a wonderfully gifted musician and speaker at our church, posed just this question to the assembled gathering one Sunday night. He challenged people to listen carefully to their hearts and then pick one of Jesus' revolutionary teachings and faithfully, courageously practice it for just one month.

WHAT IF?

> ". . .when a friend has a grudge against you—you abandon your offering and go and make things right."[1]

---

1 Matthew 5:23–24 (MSG), paraphrase

". . .you don't make your words true by embellishing them with religious lace. You just say 'yes' and 'no'."[2]

". . .when someone takes unfair advantage of you, use the occasion to practice the servant life."[3]

". . .when you give a luncheon or dinner, you invite those who can't repay you."[4]

". . .when you pray, you find a quiet, secluded place so you won't be tempted to role-play before God."[5]

". . .you give your entire attention to what God is doing right now, and don't get worked up about what may or may not happen tomorrow."[6]

". . .you give to anyone who asks you."[7]

No sooner had I picked Jesus' last statement on true generosity, than I encountered a homeless man at the end of an exit ramp, holding an Unemployed—Need Money to Feed My Family sign and a cup. What was my courageous, faith-filled response? I turned the other way, fiddled with the radio and wished the light would turn green faster. Why did I have to choose the exit ramp with a "No Turn On Red" sign?

What does God expect of us? Just this: "He's already made it

---

2 Matthew 5:37 (MSG), paraphrase
3 Matthew 5:42 (MSG)
4 Luke 14:12–14, paraphrase
5 Matthew 6:6 (MSG), paraphrase
6 Matthew 6:33 (MSG), paraphrase
7 Matthew 5:42, paraphrase

plain how to live, what to do, what God is looking for in men and women. It's quite simple: Do what is fair and just to your neighbor, be compassionate and loyal in your love, and don't take yourself too seriously—take God seriously."[8]

Taking God seriously at His word and striking out in the direction of His heartfelt call is likely to cause, at a minimum, anxiety, and more likely, deep fear—the panic that accompanies being over our head and out of control.

JESUS' UNTIMELY QUESTION

It is in just such a moment of panic for His disciples when Jesus intervenes with His seemingly untimely question. To even ask it seemed foolish. It is the question he uses to call their faith forward into a deeper level of courage and conviction. He asks the same question of us today, as we sense the restlessness of our heart to be bolder in our lives, relationships, work and faith. He asks us to step out, to take a stand, to take him at His word. It is a question he cannot answer for us: *"Why are you so afraid?"*

It was at Jesus' invitation that the disciples found themselves in such a fix in the first place. Having just completed a full day's teaching, Jesus encouraged His small band to leave the crowd behind and set out on a lake-crossing, faith-deepening journey. During the night, a sudden storm blows up and threatens to sink their small boat. Quickly overcome, the followers cry out to Jesus, who amazingly is deep asleep, either with the exhaustion that comes from giving oneself fully to others or with the peace that must accompany being the master of meteorology.

---

8 Micah 6:8 (MSG)

Jesus' question about His disciples' fear is designed to take their eyes off the furious squall that threatened to sink them and refocus them squarely back on His presence and power. In his devotional *My Utmost for His Highest,* Oswald Chambers writes of Peter's short-lived walk on top of the waves: "We step right out with recognition of God in some things, then self-consideration enters our lives and down we go. If we are truly recognizing our Lord, we have no business being concerned about how and where he engineers our circumstances. The things surrounding us are real, but when we look at them we are immediately overwhelmed and even unable to recognize Jesus. Then comes His rebuke 'Why did you doubt?' We must let our actual circumstances be what they may, but keep recognizing Jesus, maintaining complete reliance on him."[9]

What about you? Have you answered what you thought to be God's desire planted in your heart only to find the sea of your life stirred up by some sudden squall? There emerges an interesting and instructive sequence in Mark's account of how God works, forcing us to relinquish our self-reliance, confront our fear and deepen our faith.

In Chapter One, we learned that desire is the origin of faith, and the desire that God has placed in our hearts is for himself. "He has also set eternity in the hearts of men."[10] But he does not stop with mere desire. God immediately challenges us to risk it all in order that we sink down roots of faith anchored deeply in him that will not wither *when* (not *if*) the heat of life is turned up.

---

9   Oswald Chambers, *My Utmost for His Highest*
10   Ecclesiastes 3:11

Going to the other side

A consistent pattern emerges in scripture when God is preparing
to accomplish something great through His people. He always
calls them to risk—to step out so far in faith that whatever it
is they are about to attempt could never be accomplished were
he not in the center of their actions. Noah is called to build a
boat, anticipating a storm at a time when the earth had never
yet seen rain.[11] Abraham is called to slaughter his only son after
waiting for 100 years to be a father.[12] Joshua is called to cross the
Jordan River at the peak of flood season in order to take hold of
the land God promised.[13] Three men—Shadrach, Meshach and
Abednego—are called to step into a blast furnace in order to defy
the order of an ungodly leader.[14] The prostitute Rahab is called
to hide two spies sent by Joshua to explore Jericho, thereby
earning an honorable mention in Jesus' genealogy in Matthew
1.[15] Ananias is called to minister to the murderer Saul, to deliver
a sobering message of "the hard suffering that goes with (the)
job"[16] of being a Christ-follower.

Hebrews 11 is called the honor role of faith. It details the lives
of men and women who risked everything to answer God's
invitation to take him at His word and His promises. The list is
so long, that the author concludes, "I could go on and on, but
I've run out of time. There are so many more—Gideon, Barak,
Samson, Jephthah, David, Samuel, the prophets…. Through
acts of faith, they toppled kingdoms, made justice work, took

---

11 Genesis 6
12 Genesis 22
13 Joshua 3
14 Daniel 3
15 Joshua 2; Matthew 1:5
16 Acts 9:16 (MSG)

the promises for themselves. They were protected from lions, fires, and sword thrusts, turned disadvantage to advantage, won battles, routed alien armies. Women received their loved ones back from the dead." So far, so good. But the story continues, "There were those who, under torture, refused to give in and go free, preferring something better: resurrection. Others braved abuse and whips, and, yes, chains and dungeons. We have stories of those who were stoned, sawed in two, murdered in cold blood; stories of vagrants wandering the earth in animal skins, homeless, friendless, powerless—the world didn't deserve them!—making their way as best they could on the cruel edges of the world."[17] Whoops! Homeless? Friendless? Powerless? Sawed in two? Can't we just navigate the safe center rather than the "cruel edges of the world"?

All of these men and women were living out the life of godly risk described by William Barclay, who wrote, "The very essence of life is in risking life and spending life, not in saving and hoarding it. True, it is the way of weariness, of exhaustion, of giving to the uttermost, but it is better any day to burn out than to rust out, for that is the way to true joy and the way to God."[18]

Jesus invites the disciples in Mark 4 to push out from the shore and "go over to the other side."[19] This would have been no great sweat if the disciples had hugged the shoreline all the way around to the other side of the lake. Even if a strong storm blew in and they were swamped in the shallows, the disciples could merely get out and walk safely to shore. But the "other side" to which Jesus was calling them required pushing out into the deep. There was no time to be leisurely. On the other side was

17 Hebrews 11:32–38 (MSG)
18 William Barclay
19 Mark 4:35

a region inhabited by the poorest Gentiles—people who lived in caves that provided both a shelter for the living and a burial spot for the dead. Jesus was challenging His followers to leave behind superficial service to the saved in order to cross over into courageously living for the least, the lost and the left out. In the crossing was great discomfort, fear, even a panic-filled cry for rescue.

The fear caused by risk often provides an epiphany moment—a clear revelation of God intended to deepen our faith. "Search your heart for the Isaac in your life—name it—money, face, reputation, prestige, love of stuff—and then place it on the altar as an offering to the Lord, and you will know the meaning of Abrahamic trust."[20]

What is your "other side"? Who is your Isaac? Only when God breaks through our carefully erected walls of false self-sufficiency and forces us to cry out in fear to him are we ready to truly trust. God is not moved by our circumstances. He is, however, moved to action when we, like the disciples, cry out to him.

BACK TO THE BOOKS

When we choose to risk life rather than to save or hoard it, when we step into the deep waters or begin to cross over to the other side, we can expect to encounter resistance. Call it spiritual physics. Taking action for God is often met by an opposite, and even greater, reaction from Satan. When the disciples pushed out into the deep waters, a "furious squall came up."[21]

---

20 Brennan Manning, *Ruthless Trust,* 177
21 Mark 4:37

It was not the weather that was furious, but rather the forces of evil. While Jesus slept, evil was aroused. Benign Sunday-going-to-church faith meets with little opposition, spiritually or physically. Satan pays little attention to the compliant attendees of holy huddles. They represent a minor risk to him. But to step out into the deep water of courageous faith is to stir up active resistance, often in areas or relationships that are closest to us.

My friend Tom has been a faithful and wise participant in a small men's group I lead every other Friday morning. He has a diverse background as a pastor and successful business leader. His active curiosity and life shaped by raising three boys all combine to make him a wonderful and often razor-sharp-witted contributor to the biweekly dialogue.

One week our little group discussed the growing desire that several members had to move beyond our comfortable rhythm of meeting, discussing a book, praying, and catching up on each other's lives. We had engaged in a service project the previous spring, helping landscape a cloister for Carmelite monks, but had largely remained inwardly focused on supporting each other as men, fathers and businesspeople. Now, because of the confluence of several life circumstances, a number of the guys were feeling called to take a bolder step into our collective faith journey. They actually wanted to consistently *do* something with their faith.

We discussed several options, from feeding street people to building homes for the homeless to supporting the education needs of women in rural Africa. However, several of the men voiced a frightening belief that if we stepped out in faithful acts of service, we would likely encounter additional resistance. In my own faith journey, I have experienced a God who is messy and unpredictable. I have come to know him more through struggle and spiritual wrestling during the night than through the bright sunshine of success. For many of the men in our group as well, God is more a God of questions asked in the depths of pain and uncertainty than a God of simple answers offered in times of a life on cruise control.

Our group discussed the resistance that would likely push up against our bold intentions of faithful service, and then committed to spending the next two weeks in prayer, waiting on God to clarify His desire for our actions.

The very next Tuesday, Tom was summoned to his manager's office and informed that he was being fired at will (he was quickly and completely exonerated from any shred of causality). He was escorted to his office by HR, given five minutes to clear out his personal possessions, and then ushered permanently out of the building and the company. Tom called me in tears from his car on the way home—confused, disoriented, humiliated, angry and afraid—but sensing intuitively a direct connection between the bold pursuit of our group and this devastating life event. After relaying the dizzying events he had just experienced, his simple question was, "Can we just go back to reading books?" Of course, at this point the genie had left the bottle. It was too late to recork our God-inspired desire to serve. As time would reveal, however, Tom's experience would draw him and our whole group into much deeper water than we ever anticipated or desired. The result was a far richer relationship with God in all of our individual faith journeys.

It would be much easier and safer to remain lukewarm, uncommitted and risk-averse in our faith so as to avoid the pain of crossing over to the other side. But it is just this attitude for which God reserves some of His most stinging judgment: "I know you inside and out, and find little to my liking. You're not cold, you're not hot—far better to be either cold or hot! You're stale. You're stagnant. You make me want to vomit. You brag, 'I'm rich, I've got it made, I need nothing from anyone,' oblivious that in fact you're a pitiful, blind beggar, threadbare and homeless."[22] God's harshest judgment is for the sins of *omission* (when we fail to act) than the sins of *commission* (when we act but screw it up).

Tom learned from his experience of being fired that, "God grabbed me by the throat of my passive belief, claimed me, and made me declare my life for him. He revealed himself to me in a personal way that pierced my self-reliance, my need for status and my need for others' approval as being the most important things to me. Beyond all of this, God reassured me with the most profound learning—to stop being afraid!" God had called Tom to name the Isaacs of his life and sacrifice them on the altar of his unemployment.

No risk, no reward. But in between risk and reward is fearfully strong resistance. Count on it.

> **Resistance is often the confirmation that we are in the sweet spot of God's will. Our greatest fear should not be that we encounter resistance. Our greatest fear is that we succeed at something that does not matter to God. Perhaps the amount of resistance encountered is the gauge that registers the degree to which God celebrates our success.**

---

22   Revelation 3:15–17 (MSG)

God's with-ness

The reward for faithful risk is God's *with-ness*, especially in times of overwhelming resistance. St. Bernard Parish was among the hardest hit communities ravaged by Hurricane Katrina. The storm killed 114 people in St. Bernard and flooded every one of its 24,000 homes. The storm surge hit at 10:00 a.m. on August 29, 2005, and took only 15 minutes to cover the parish in over 10 feet of water.

Dorothy Hingle lit a candle sometime after 9:00 a.m. in her small brick house on Rosetta Street and prayed. She always lit a candle when she prayed. Dorothy spent her entire life in St. Bernard. At age 83 she was the matriarch of her large family of 5 children, 15 grandchildren, 41 great-grandchildren and 10 great-great-grandchildren. Most of her time was devoted to caring for her 54-year-old stepson, Russell Embry, who had been paralyzed and severely brain injured in a 1974 accident. For 31 years, Dorothy had served as Russell's primary caregiver, bathing, feeding and cleaning up after him.

Widowed in 1992, Dorothy had begun to be slowed by arthritis. She gave up driving and enlisted the help of others in caring for Russell. So complete was her devotion, however, that she seldom left his side, even to go to the grocery store.

Russell was 6'4" tall and weighed about 250 pounds. As a result, he was on a special-needs list for those who needed to be evacuated in the event of a hurricane. As Katrina approached, Dorothy made arrangements for the ambulance to evacuate Russell and her just as she had done in past storms. As the rest of the family fled, Dorothy assured them that "The ambulance is coming to get us. They're coming now. Don't worry about us."

God is *with* us."

After Katrina's waters inundated St. Bernard Parish, there was no word from Dorothy or Russell. For the next 24 days, the family frantically searched hospitals, nursing homes and the Internet for them. They supplied DNA samples and posted descriptions on 40 Web sites praying all the while that the ambulance had arrived in time.

As the water receded, searchers found Dorothy and Russell in their small brick home on Rosetta Street. Her purse was by the door in anticipation of her escape. The small candle was next to her with the wax that flowed out when the floodwaters washed over it. Dorothy and Russell died just as they had lived for 31 years—together. They lay together in Russell's bed with Dorothy's arms wrapped tightly around him, refusing in the face of the rising floodwaters to let go. God's grip on Dorothy strengthened her grip on Russell.

If anyone had occasion to flee in the face of the rising waters of resistance, it was the apostle Paul. Wrenched from a career of killing followers of Jesus into a calling to reach the cave dwellers of his day, he endured whippings, shipwrecks, betrayals, stoning, hunger, and the desertion of earthly brothers in the name of Jesus for his efforts. In spite (or perhaps because) of all this, Paul was so completely confident of God as the eternal reward for his risk that he states, "I'm absolutely convinced that nothing— nothing living or dead, angelic or demonic, today or tomorrow, high or low, thinkable or unthinkable—absolutely *nothing* can get between us and God's love because of the way that Jesus our Master has embraced us."[23] The reward for risking is God's all-

---

23   Romans 8:38–39 (MSG), italics added

powerful grip on us. Nothing, nothing, nothing can cause him to let go. *Why are we so afraid?*

While God's grasp never weakens, we must let go of all our excuses and distractions in order to wholeheartedly live out our faith. This is why Jesus knew he had to ask us the next question to enlarge our faith, a question intended to diagnose our spiritual health: *"Do you want to get well?"*

Chapter Two

WHY ARE YOU SO AFRAID?

READ
the following Scripture:
- Hebrews 11
- Romans 8:38–39

REFLECT
on the following questions:
1. What is the "other side" for you?
2. Where have you encountered resistance as you attempt to practice a bolder faith?
3. When have you felt God's *with-ness* in your life?

RESPOND
to the following challenge:
- Choose one of Jesus' revolutionary teachings and practice it for 30 days. Share with one other person the impact this has on your faith.

CHAPTER 3

Do You Want to Get Well?

WHOLENESS

Some time later, Jesus went up to Jerusalem for a feast of the Jews. Now there is in Jerusalem near the Sheep Gate a pool, which in Aramaic is called Bethesda and which is surrounded by five covered colonnades. Here a great number of disabled people used to lie—the blind, the lame, the paralyzed—and they waited for the moving of the waters. From time to time an angel of the Lord would come down and stir up the waters. The first one into the pool after each such disturbance would be cured of whatever disease he had. One who was there had been an invalid for thirty-eight years. When Jesus saw him lying there and learned that he had been in this condition for a long time, he asked him,

"Do you want to get well?"

John 5:1–6

Do You Want to Get Well?

WILL I EVER FEEL HEALTHY AGAIN?

Carol had been ill for over three months. What had begun as a slight discomfort in her lower abdomen had progressed to constant pain, rendering her unable to go about the active and healthy life with which she had been blessed for 48 years. Simple daily tasks required more energy than she could muster. Her work as a nurse in an ophthalmology clinic became day-to-day pending her energy and degree of pain. Carol considered taking a leave of absence rather than put the clinic in a daily quandary over her availability.

With her background in medicine and nearly two decades' experience in nursing, Carol is as good an advocate for her personal health as anyone I know. She asks the tough questions and speaks the mysterious language of medicine. Carol doggedly pursues doctors, nurses and appointment schedulers until she successfully gets answers. In her lowest and most vulnerable moments, however, Carol was beginning to doubt that she would ever resume a healthy, pain-free life. She was facing the possibility that she was in this diminished state of being for the long haul—possibly for life. When the deep discouragement of unanswered prayer washed over her, she cried out, "Will I ever feel healthy again?"

At no time during her ordeal did any of the physicians, specialists, nurses, lab technicians, orderlies, residents or helpers turn to Carol and ask, "Do you want to get well?" To ask such a question would be somewhere on a scale between astonishingly insensitive and deeply disrespectful. What person, when dealing with a chronic, debilitating condition would *not* want to be restored to full health? Carol's constant prayer was for an immediate and full recovery. She was joined in that prayer by countless friends and family. No one would ever conceive of questioning her desire for healing.

JESUS' UNTHINKABLE QUESTION

In His perfect grasp of the wholeness of every life story, however, Jesus asked just that question, "Do you want to get well?"[1] At the height of one of the Pilgrimage Feasts requiring all Jewish males to venture to Jerusalem, Jesus steps into the center of the suffering beggars of Bethesda and stuns a long-suffering man with His unthinkable question. He had the audacity to question the desire of a man who "had been an invalid for thirty-eight years."[2] Thirty-eight years! For almost four decades this man had been huddled with the hundreds of "sick people—blind, crippled, paralyzed"[3]—in the alcoves of the Sheep Gate pool of Jerusalem. The belief was that periodically an angel of the Lord would come down, ripple the water and then watch the mad dash for healing. The first person into the pool after the Holy ripple would be cured of whatever ailed him. In the interim, the hundreds of alcove-dwellers would beg their daily subsistence from passersby.

Perhaps the invalid trusted the healing power of rippling water more than the righteous power of an Almighty God. Maybe he would rather have remained a comfortable beggar than a courageous kingdom-maker. Rather than *reaching out*, the invalid

---

1 John 5:6
2 John 5:5
3 John 5:3 (MSG)

had become accustomed to *pressing in* to the shadowy recesses of the alcoves. He remained huddled with the hundreds of other forgotten and ailing men and women who had given in to the despair of long-unanswered prayers or to the predictability of subsistence living supported by the charity of passersby. But Jesus was about to transform all of this with His one unthinkable question: "Do you want to get well?"

Jesus was willing to give the invalid the opportunity to remain impaired. He had to answer Jesus' question for himself, as do we. My friend Tom e-mailed me his thoughts on Jesus' question. "He seemed to be asking, 'Are you sure that you are ready to have a radical redirection in your life? All of your excuses will be gone. Your limitations henceforth will be self-inflicted. You will have a world of new opportunities, new challenges, new demands and new joys. Are you sure you're ready to leave your familiar and move into a new state of being?'"

What about you? Do *you* want to get well? Are you ready for a new state of being?

Webster's New World Dictionary defines *invalid* in the following ways:

> in•val•id: 1.) Not well; weak; sickly; infirm; chronically ill or disabled 2.) To remove from active duty or retire because of ill health 3.) Not valid—having no face; null or void[4]

Are you feeling weak in body or spirit? Have you removed yourself from "active duty," choosing to press into the shadows of

---

4 Webster's New World Dictionary, 740

seclusion and self-sufficiency rather than step out into the light of community and commitment? Are you feeling as if you have no influence, no voice—as if your life right now is somehow of little value or effect?

Perhaps by no more than the fluke of alphabetical positioning, the word that appears directly below *invalid* in the dictionary is *invaluable*.

> in•valu•able: 1.) Having value too great to
> measure 2.) Priceless[5]

None of us are invalids in God's eyes, but rather invaluables. True, we may indeed be sick or weak in body, crippled by debilitating disease or even approaching death. We may be chronically ill in spirit with patterns of self-defeating behavior that we cannot shake on our own, but we are priceless to God— of a value too great to measure.

We are the one lost sheep he hunts down to the exclusion of the 99 others who require no such rescue.[6] We are the lost coin that he searches frantically for, turning over the whole house.[7] We are the lost sons that he stands in wait for and rushes madly to hug when we stumble home. He throws massive parties on our behalf, clothes us in the royal finery and kills the best in the herd for us—just for showing back up.[8] These story lines all move us deeply because we hunger to be loved, to be valued in such a way. And we are! We are so priceless that God offers up His most valuable asset—His only Son, Jesus, on our behalf in order to

---

5   Webster's New World Dictionary, 740

6   Luke 15:1–7

7   Luke 15:8–10

8   Luke 15:11–32

restore us to a love relationship and demonstrate our measureless value to him. Invalid? No way! Invaluable? Without a doubt!

But this is a challenging truth in which to live daily. We get sucked into believing the lies perpetrated by slick marketing that we somehow just do not measure up. We slip back into timid, fear-filled behavior or wither in the face of disease. We limp along at half speed or curl up halfheartedly in the shadows of the alcove. It is all so much easier than saying "yes" to a radical redirection.

There emerges in Jesus' question about our health a rhythm of godly healing, not just of body but also of mind, spirit and soul. There is His initial command to "get up"—to take action, to stop lying in the shadows, but to stand up, leaning on His steadying hand. There is His encouragement to "pick up"—to pick up only what we can carry, leaving behind all the baggage of wasted years, futile efforts and fruitless self-dependence. We are to pick up only our mat, perhaps as a reminder of once being sick but restored now to wholeness.

Finally, there is His expectation that we "speak up." We are always healed for a purpose—blessed to be a blessing. Our own healing is so that we become the arms and legs of the Greatest Healer.

The restoration of Carol's health began with a caring Mayo Clinic physician's question, "What is your story? Start at the beginning." Jesus skips right by this pleasantry with the invalid and with us. Being there from the beginning[9] and the author of each of our stories, he cuts to the chase with His penetrating question, "Do

---

9 John 1:1

you want to get well?" Jesus asks the question but cannot answer it for us. We need to weigh in for ourselves.

GET UP

God's healing begins with a command to "get up." The miracle of healing in John 5 is one of the few recorded in Scripture *not* initiated by an audacious act of faith. The healing at the pool, along with the miracle at Nain in Luke 7, stands in sharp contrast as one where Jesus did the initiating.

Jesus wanted to demonstrate that a small faith places no limits on His large plans, that knowing him intimately is not a prerequisite for being healed by him deeply. In fact, sometimes we come to know God most intimately as a result of being shocked by His healing. When we have tapped out our own initiative, exhausted our own reserves, and doctor after doctor has raised her eyebrows and shrugged his shoulders in perplexed confusion, God steps in with His perfect timing and touches us with His gentle hand of Almighty healing. Sometimes our faith stumbles to catch up to our prayers.

We must, however, be willing to break through our own spiritual inertia. If we are content to stay where we are, no healing can take place. "The power of God never dispenses with human effort. Nothing is truer than that we must realize our own helplessness; but in a very real sense, it is true that miracles happen when our will and God's power co-operate to make them possible."[10]

---

10   William Barclay, *The Gospel of John*, 209

PLAYING SMALL

"Are you as big as you want to be?" This pointed question was asked in a chance encounter with Blair, the CEO of one of our firm's clients. Caught a bit off guard by his directness, I popped in the mental tape from which I often describe our company's business design and began giving him my rote answers. This time, however, they just did not ring quite true. I sounded hollow to myself. We had somehow become accustomed to accepting our smallness. We even regularly described our firm as "small by design," as if this were a key distinguishing characteristic. Truth be told, we all desired to play and work bigger but lacked the vision, resources, wisdom, or even courage to grow beyond our self-imposed boundaries. As a result, we were certainly small but by default, not design. We were doing great work with select clients but lacked the scale to truly transform large numbers of people or whole global organizations.

God does not want us small by default. And this is certainly not His design. Militant modesty is not a God thing! Paul's encouragement to Timothy is God's instruction to us as well: "For this reason I remind you to fan into flame the gift of God, which is in you through the laying on of my hands. For God did not give us a spirit of timidity, but a spirit of power, of love and of self-discipline."[11]

Jesus contrasts the desire of the thief (Satan), who "comes only to steal and kill and destroy," with His own ministry purpose: "I have come that they may have life, and have it to the full."[12] The thief's principal trick is to have us waste time—God's and ours—by playing small. The abundant life promised by Jesus

---

11 2 Timothy 1:6–7
12 John 10:10

is not necessarily a wealth of possessions but the overflow of influence—for God's sake. "Jesus understood His purpose was to save us not from pain and suffering, but from meaninglessness."[13] It is a big life he has in mind for us.

All of this requires that we first get up, that we break free from our comfort with whatever is shackling our spirit. To get up is an act of faith and hope. We must have faith that God will steady our atrophied spirit, shriveled from disuse. And we must have hope that the life to which we are called is greater than the one we leave behind.

PICK UP

God's command to get up is followed by His encouragement to pick up—to pick up our mat and walk. Why? If we no longer need our mat because God mercifully heals us, why not leave it behind for the next poor beggar? Is God just being an environmentalist, not wanting the poolside littered by the discarded mats of healed invalids? Or does he know in His wisdom that we will need a reminder of our sickness that was transformed to significance?

Fourteen years ago, at the wise encouragement of another father, I began taking 1:1 adventures with both of our boys at least once each year. They have a chance to help plan and even pay a little bit, and we go off for several days of face-to-face, heart-to-heart, father-son time. It has become a vital part of the story of our relationship and the source of many belly laughs over the years! The first such adventure was a backpacking trip with Brett in the Holy Cross Wilderness of Colorado. Neither of us knew how to

---

13 Erwin McManus, *The Barbarian Way*, 31

read a compass. I will never forget the scene in our living room as we laid out all the things we thought we required for our inaugural four-day foray into the backcountry—food (lots of it), clothes, first aid kit, tent, sleeping bags, stove, rope, bug spray, flashlights—you get the picture. When we divided the stash and stuffed it all into our packs, they each weighed about 60 pounds. As I struggled to hoist Brett's pack onto his back, he looked at me with pleading eyes, suggesting that a hotel adventure was the way to go! We clearly needed to winnow down what we intended to carry or we would be crushed by the weight of our packs about 30 steps from the car.

If we are going to be able to answer God's command to get up, we need to check out what we are carrying. The excess baggage of wasted years, futile efforts at self-healing and help or fruitless self-dependence are not trip essentials. They weigh us down, threatening to crush us as we venture out from the shadows of the alcove into the light of a divinely healed life.

The things taking up space in our backpacks and our hearts can come in many forms—money, relationships, work, busyness, the guilt of the past, worries of the present or fear of the future. Anything that steals our heart away from faith weighs us down in our venture for God. Jesus began His ministry with an invitation to His disciples and to us to "come, follow me"[14] and ends it with the powerful command to "go...."[15] We can neither answer His invitation nor obey His command if we are frozen in our tracks by the weight of self-imposed burdens. We must be able to pick up our mat.

---

14 Matthew 4:19
15 Matthew 28:19

The word for mat in the story of the beggar is *Krabbates*, translated to mean "pallet." A pallet can have two quite different definitions, both applicable in our healing by God.

> pal•let: 1.) A platform for storing or transporting materials 2.) A wooden tool used by potters for smoothing or rounding[16]

In the account of John 5, the first definition applies. Others brought the invalid on a pallet to and from the pool on a daily basis. It was his only mode of transportation until Jesus intervened. But now his transportation was to become a tool in the hands of the Master Potter. Jesus used the pallet to shape the faith of the beggar—from invalid to invaluable, rounding off the dings and scuffs of 38 years so as to be holy art for others to witness.

HEALED TO BE A HEALER

We are healed always for a purpose—blessed to be a blessing. I continue to be reminded of this vital truth in our Friday guys group. God has brought together twelve men who have the perfect stories and life experiences to be able to minister to each other in moments of darkness and need. But it requires that we speak up.

Several years ago, in a moment of parenting despair, I reluctantly and tearfully shared my feelings of fear, anger and confusion with the group. Roger responded that he had asked his 18-year-old son to leave their house just the evening before. His son was near the bottom of a many-year struggle with drugs that was

---

16 Webster's New World Dictionary, 1022

killing him and destroying the rest of the family. Returning late from a West Coast business trip, Roger felt compelled to kick his son out onto the street rather than allow him to continue to poison the family with his drug-induced, dangerous and erratic behavior. Roger shared his story, admitting that the group was the last place he wanted to be that particular Friday morning. But he felt called by some odd force to be there—compelled despite a fear-filled, sleepless night. When I began to share my story, the reason for Roger's attendance became evident. He was there to speak hope into my despair and solidarity into my feeling of being all alone. One by one, several other men shared stories of how they too had reached moments of pain, fear, anger and confusion with their teenage sons. They also shared examples of how those defeats had become victories with time. As we were leaving that morning, wrung out by the gripping stories of difficult life experiences but bolstered by the prayers and love of each other, one of the men pulled me aside and softly said, "John, we just became a group today."

We had been meeting for years—reading, praying, telling stories, complaining about the local sports teams—but seldom speaking up with real courage or transparency about the highs and lows of our lives until that morning. Speaking up opened the floodgates of reality. When we set down the façade of lives lived in relative order and daily calm and began to share the truth, we began to become the group that God intended all along for us to be. He knit us together for just that morning— and for many more. Over the last four years, jobs have been lost, health has wavered and our faith has staggered—in other words, life has happened! And in every circumstance, there has been more than one man who has experienced, or was currently experiencing, exactly the same reality. God's expectation is that we speak up with words of hope and comfort in these exact moments. "As iron sharpens iron, so one man sharpens another."[17]

Paul was specifically chosen by Jesus himself to take the Gospel beyond the Jewish nation. His credentials were dubious at best—by his own admission he was once "a blasphemer and a persecutor and a violent man."[18] He stood by and watched as men stoned the Jesus-follower Stephen to death, a vision that was likely replayed in Paul's mind for the rest of his life. For just this very reason, Paul had a depth of understanding that translated into a passion for speaking up that just would not be quenched or quelled. "Christ Jesus came into the world to save sinners—of whom I am the worst. But for that very reason I was shown mercy so that in me, the worst of sinners, Christ Jesus might display his unlimited patience as an example to those who would believe on him and receive eternal life."[19] Or as Eugene Peterson states in *The Message*, "now he shows me off—evidence of his endless patience—to those who are right on the edge of trusting him forever."[20] Paul was blessed to be a blessing.

God commands us to get up. He encourages us to pick up. Finally, because of His healing of us, he expects us to speak up. "He comes alongside us when we go through hard times, and before you know it he brings *us* alongside someone else who is going through hard times so that we can be there for that person just as God was there for us."[21] It begins with our answer to His question, "Do you want to get well?"

---

17 Proverbs 27:17
18 1 Timothy 1:13
19 1 Timothy 1:15–16
20 1 Timothy 1:16 (MSG)
21 2 Corinthians 1:4 (MSG), italics added

Given our own healing, why would we limp along, hiding behind the pseudonyms of a previous life rather than boldly proclaim our true identity as a follower of Jesus? Jesus confronts a demon-possessed man with *"What is your name?"* to call out our true identity and challenge us to step fully into our role as active members of His holy family.

Chapter Three

DO YOU WANT TO GET WELL?

READ
the following Scripture:
- Luke 15:1–32
- 1 Timothy 1:12–17 (Preferably in *The Message*)

REFLECT
on the following questions:
1. Where are you currently "playing small" in your life, work and/or faith?
2. What is currently weighing you down in your life and faith journey?
3. To whom are you feeling called to minister?

RESPOND
to the following challenge:
- Inventory what you are carrying in your "backpack" the next 30 days and determine what, if anything—money, relationships, work, busyness, the guilt of the past, worries about the present, or fear of the future—is weighing you down in your pursuit of God and of others. Commit to sharing this inventory with one other person in an effort to rebalance your load.

What Is Your Name?

IDENTITY

They sailed to the region of the Gerasenes, which is across the lake from Galilee. When Jesus stepped ashore, he was met by a demon-possessed man from town. For a long time this man had not worn clothes or lived in a house, but had lived in the tombs. When he saw Jesus, he cried out and fell at his feet, shouting at the top of his voice, "What do you want with me, Jesus, Son of the Most High God? I beg you, don't torture me!" For Jesus had commanded the evil spirit to come out of the man. Many times it had seized him, and though he was chained hand and foot and kept under guard, he had broken his chains and had been driven by the demon into solitary places. Jesus asked him,

"What is your name?"

Luke 8:26–30

What Is Your Name?

Monty's relational tapestry

On the first night of every new class he taught, Monty would require the completion of a biographical form including contact information and a family photo. One entire wall in his cramped office was covered with photos of students. They were beginning to spill over to the adjoining walls. Black, white, brown; young, old; female, male; singles, couples, families; healthy, frail—a visual tapestry representing decades of deep investment in the lives of others.

I received a preview of the kind of relationship I was to enjoy with him when I turned in my first form and family portrait. The picture had been taken on a breathtakingly beautiful day somewhere in the Cascade Mountains. Because of the glare off of the glacier, we were all wearing sunglasses. Monty looked at the picture, then up at me, inquiring with a mischievous grin, "Are you all in the witness protection program?"

What began as a nine-month Bible Survey class blossomed over thirteen years into the richest of friendships with Monty and, consequently, with God. Every time I would meet with Monty, he would pepper me with questions about my life, work, family and faith. Often, the questions would come rapid-fire, five at a time, without even the courtesy of a pause for answers. Invariably, however, within the first two or three, he would put his finger directly on something deep within my soul. Whether a passion, hurt, desire, doubt or regret, Monty had a divine, unique gift of revealing what was hidden, ignored or barely scabbed over.

I asked him on one occasion how he knew to ask the specific

question that had on that day uncovered a long unspoken fear. He replied that he had been praying for hours before I had shown up—prayed for me, by name—while looking at my family photo. These laser-guided prayers granted permission for dark to become light and anonymity to become known.

There was no witness protection program or any other kind of protection program with Monty. If you dared sit down with him, you had best be prepared to be opened up by spiritual exploratory surgery. God's Word was the scalpel, and penetrating questions were his technique. Monty's inquiries quickly revealed both the reality of my situation and my true identity. I always left our times together with newfound clarity.

Jesus' revealing question

After a long day of telling stories to teach timeless truths, Jesus challenged His closest followers to join him on a journey to the other side.[1] While the crowd remained on the shore, the little group set out to cross the Sea of Galilee at night. Given that several of Jesus' followers were professional fishermen, the night crossing of a notoriously fickle body of water was not the boldest part of Jesus' challenge. They knew how to handle a boat. The risk was not so much what they were doing, it was where they were going. The little band was crossing over from the devoutly Jewish region that had produced 4 of the 12 disciples to the poorest of Gentile regions. Eugene Peterson describes their destination as being "directly opposite Galilee."[2] This could not have been truer, geographically or spiritually.

---

1 Mark 4:35
2 Luke 8:26 (MSG)

If the storm that almost drowned them en route was not enough to set off a panic attack, the group arrived at night to a welcome reception featuring a naked man screaming at the top of his voice with chains hanging off his arms and legs. It is a scene straight out of a Stephen King novel, designed to get directly at the core of where the disciples placed their faith. What could be worse for a Jew than being in an unclean burial ground at night, confronted by a naked man who dwelled with the dead, while surrounded by rooting pigs?

The setting was horror movie perfect, but the story does not follow the predictable script. Three phenomena distinguish this most unusual encounter, all of which reveal the focus of our own faith. First, despite the creepiest of settings, Jesus appears perfectly calm. Surprisingly, the demons are terrified. As was the case in the fierce storm during the lake crossing, Jesus remains bold and unruffled. Because he is so in step with His Father—"I and the Father are one heart and mind"[3]—Jesus is fully confident that he confronts evil with all of heaven having His back. Do we access the same power by seeking the same solidarity?

Second, and equally astonishing, is the fact that even during this initial encounter, the demons know Jesus by name. After years of intimate friendship and daily walks of faith, the closest followers of Jesus still had to be prompted with the question, "Who do *you* say that I am?"[4] This was not so with the mob of evil occupying the naked grave dweller. They immediately confront Jesus by name and by the rightful place he occupies in the universe— "Son of the High God."[5] His enemies are on a first-name basis with Jesus. Are we?

3 John 10:30 (MSG)
4 Luke 9:20, italics added
5 Luke 8:28 (MSG)

Third, perhaps the most disconcerting turn of events was that Jesus' first attempt at driving out the demons seemingly failed. This must have pulled His followers up short! Didn't Jesus just muzzle a storm with one word merely an hour earlier? The followers likely feared he had used up all His juice on the lake! They had seen Jesus issue strong orders and drive out demons on every prior occasion, but this time, it did not appear to be working. Are we fully confident in God's resolve to always triumph over evil?

Jesus employed a means he used throughout history and still uses today to call out our true identity and refocus our faith. He asks, *"What is your name?"*

What an odd question! If you were staring into the face of evil in a dark graveyard at night, would you want to introduce yourself? Wouldn't you think that the creator of the universe,[6] the God who has our hairs numbered[7] and knows the flight path of every sparrow[8] could remember a name? I am terrible at names! Shouldn't God be better?

Jesus asks, "What is your name?" not as a means of prodding His faulty memory, but as His divine methodology of reversing *our* flimsy embrace of so many false identities. He already knows our name. He wants *us* to become acquainted, perhaps for the first time, with *our* Royal identity. The demon-racked man in the graveyard had a whole Roman legion—6,000—of false identities holding him hostage.

---

6 Genesis 14:19
7 Matthew 10:30
8 Matthew 10:29

LIVING WITH ALIASES

The world's population is roughly 6.6 billion people. You may have seen this breakdown of demographics assuming that the world were a village of 100 people:

- 61 villagers would be Asian (of that, 20 would be Chinese and 17 would be Indian), 14 would be African, 11 would be European, 9 would be Latin or South American, 5 would be North American.
- 18 villagers would be unable to read or write, but 33 would have cell phones and 16 would be online on the Internet.
- 27 villagers would be under 15 years of age, and 7 would be over 64 years old.
- There would be an equal number of males and females.
- There would be 18 cars in the village.
- 63 villagers would have inadequate sanitation.
- 33 villagers would be Christian, 20 would be Muslim, 13 would be Hindus, 6 would be Buddhist, 2 would be Atheists, 12 would be nonreligious and the remaining 14 would be members of other religions.
- 30 villagers would be unemployed or under employed, while of the 70 who do work, 28 work in agriculture, 14 would work in industry and the remaining 28 would work in the service sector. 53 villagers would live on less than two U.S. dollars a day.
- One villager would have AIDS, 26 villagers would smoke, and 14 villagers would be obese.

What stunned me is that 67 villagers would have no identity. Of the 6.6 billion people in the world, 4.4 billion are unknown in the sense that they have no published name, social security number, street address or bank account. About 8.3 million adults were victims of identity theft in 2005. The 4.4 billion unknowns were not among them because there is nothing to steal. From a legal standpoint, it is as if they do not exist.

There are times when I choose to be unknown. If I have been out all day or all week with people, I treasure being able to merely participate in something while letting others take the lead. I enjoy running and biking alone. This allows me to recharge and refresh. This is both a natural and healthy means for me to recover my energy.

Remaining anonymous can become unhealthy, however. "Many of us live our lives making sure we are not seen. We choose the cloak of invisibility. We choose to remain uninvolved, and our love for personal privacy disguises both our indifference and our isolation."[9] We hang back not out of a desire to refuel but out of apathy or laziness.

The man in Luke's account was neither choosing healthy anonymity nor personal indifference. He "had been driven...into solitary places"[10] by his demons. This is one of the Evil One's prevalent schemes—to make us feel all alone, lacking any name or voice. We feel as if we are unknown even to the Almighty. Satan has been at this game a very long time. He has it down cold and, consequently, so do we.

Consider the ancient story of Elijah. In one of the most stunning reversals in all of Scripture, the prophet goes from the pinnacle of public victory to the pit of private isolation in just one chapter. You perhaps know the story. Elijah challenges the whole people

---

9   Erwin Raphael McManus, *Chasing Daylight,* 135
10 Luke 8:29

of Israel along with 850 prophets to declare their allegiance to the god who is able to rain down fire on an altar of wood and a sacrificial bull.

The prophets pray all morning. No answer. Elijah engages in some godly trash-talking, "Call a little louder—he is a god, after all. Maybe he's off meditating somewhere or other, or maybe he's gotten involved in a project, or maybe he's on vacation. You don't suppose he's overslept, do you, and needs to be waked up?"[11] Nothing. Not a spark.

Then Elijah steps up, repairs the altar with twelve stones representing all of the tribes of Israel, cuts his sacrificial bull into pieces, and soaks everything with water until it fills the surrounding trench. In a culminating act that would make even a televangelist blush, Elijah calls but once on God to make His name known. Immediately, God's fire consumes the offering, wood, stones, dirt and all of the water in the moat.

The people repent. The false prophets are slaughtered. God wins. Evil loses. Elijah runs off into the sunset, basking in the glory of victory. End of story. Until…we next catch up with him sitting under a tree contemplating suicide and slipping into the deep slumber of depression. What happened?

In the space of only one chapter, the Evil One, seemingly defeated on the mountaintop, was making a remarkable comeback. He had isolated Elijah and had him convinced that he was "the only one left"[12] among all of the followers of God.

---

11 1 Kings 18:27 (MSG)
12 1 Kings 19:10

Before I become too self-righteous with the followers of the false prophets or judgmental about the doubts of Elijah, I need to recall my own experience. I have to admit that I have felt the despair of unanswered prayer, even when reaching out to the real God. It has seemed, as with Elijah's taunts, that God was busy with other projects or taking an extended time away. I can recall many times crying out to God for a divine solution or powerful act and seemingly hearing back exactly nothing! Satan had me all alone without even the lifeline of prayer, or so it seemed.

Much was made of the recently published biography *Mother Teresa: Come Be My Light*. Many were shocked to learn that Mother Teresa spent the last half century of her life tormented by the sense that God had abandoned her. She describes her spiritual health using words like "dryness" and "torture," finding only "darkness and coldness and emptiness so great that nothing touches my soul."[13] Like Elijah, she descended from the pinnacle of making God's love tangible to the sick and dying of Calcutta into the abyss of emptiness and isolation. Mother Teresa felt alone even as the religious order she founded prospered.

To be sure, there are times that God calls His most faithful followers into what St. John of the Cross vividly describes as "the dark night of the soul." The purpose of such a period is not to shackle us with fear, but rather to free us for service. "What does the dark night of the soul involve? We may have a sense of dryness, aloneness, even lostness. Any over dependence on the emotional life is stripped away. The dark night is one of the ways God brings us into a hush, a stillness so that he may work an inner transformation upon the soul."[14]

---

13   Kenneth L. Woodward, "A Special Breed of Saint" in the *Wall Street Journal*,
14   Richard J. Foster, *Celebration of Discipline*, 102

It was during Elijah's isolation that God calls to him, speaking in "a gentle and quiet whisper."[15]

God asks, to paraphrase the popular cell phone commercial, "Can you hear me now?" Whether we are isolated by Satan's scheming or by God's governance, we need to hear the gentle and quiet whisper in order to escape our anonymity. Have you heard God's whisper lately?

My friend Keith recently commented that I was truly blessed to have had Monty as a "spiritual soul mate" for thirteen years. I wish he had left it at that. Keith continued by challenging me to aspire to a similar role in the lives of others, taking on the mantle of mentorship.

God was whispering through Keith, inviting me to step out of anonymity into a new identity as a lover and soul mate of others. But here is the rub. My life's business card is already crammed with the identities of husband, father, family member, friend, business owner, churchgoer, small group leader, and so on. I would rather hide behind all of these other worthy identities than assume another challenging role.

The 4.4 billion unknowns are all intimately known by God, as are we. Fortunately, with God we are never anonymous, never without character or lacking a name, never truly isolated. We may, however, have far too many aliases that interfere with the true identity to which we are called.

---

15 1 Kings 19:12 (MSG)

WHAT IS YOUR TRAIN NAME?

Tom is one of the most creative men I know, so it came as no surprise that when I asked him for a business card at the end of a lunch meeting, he asked, "Which one?" and then produced three. It was a little unexpected, however, that the third card had a completely different name and title!

Recalling Monty's question, I teasingly inquired, "Are you in the witness protection program?" "Oh, no," he replied, "that's just my train name." I can honestly say I had never heard that reply before. It begged the rest of the story, which Tom was happy to supply several weeks later over a cup of coffee.

Tom decided when he was 29 to jump a freight train to the West Coast with two friends. They began on a full-moon evening in July of 1986, and rode boxcars from Minnesota to North Dakota, through Montana to Washington, finally ending up three days later in Seattle.

Adding to their epic journey, the three buddies assumed train names and fictitious professions. John, a retail broker, assumed his childhood nickname Jocko, later shortened to Ock, and became an unemployed hockey coach. Brian, a lawyer, became Spike, the writer. My friend Tom, an accountant, became Dusty. He later added his mom's maiden name Herold. His assumed profession was a photographer.

Why would the train name assumed by a 29-year-old adventurer still occupy the business card of a now 50-year-old business owner? Tom has succeeded at virtually everything he has tried in his professional life. He became a CPA in a Big Four accounting firm and was an owner, manufacturer, distributor, president and

CEO of salon businesses in Minneapolis, Denver, New York City and Italy. He currently owns a consulting practice.

Along the way, Tom began to actively pursue his fictitious train profession of photographer. Using his pseudonym of Dusty Herold, he submitted pictures to the newsletter of his own salon company and began to exhibit an original collection of photos called the "Shadow Man."

When I inquired why he chose to disguise his true identity, Tom's answer was direct: "No one would have taken me seriously. To them, I was 'Tom the accountant.'" His fear was that the amazing photographic narrative "Shadow Man" would somehow be diminished by his everyday identity of accountant, consultant or even CEO.

How many identities do you carry around? I go by many, depending on the situation. I am the husband of Carol and the father of two twenty-something sons, Brett and Joshua. Add on business owner, brother, family member, son, churchgoer, small group leader, community member and friend. But it does not end there! I am also hiker, climber, runner, cyclist, reader, traveler and many more. There is no font size small enough to fit all of these identities on one business card. I am tugged daily in many different directions by each of these identities. Having this many roles inherently creates conflict among them for investment of time, energy, even money. Don't get me wrong. These are wonderful identities. I am truly blessed to carry all of them. But they are all "train names," not the most important identity to which I am called.

What is your family name?

It always causes me to think when I have to fill out the immigration form while traveling outside the U.S. The form asks first for my surname—my family name—and then for all of the given names from my passport. Given names represent a voluntary choice and often capture the hopes, dreams and desired character of a family. We can have numerous given names, but only one family name. And it is our family name by which God calls us.

"'But now, God's Message, the God who made you in the first place, Jacob, the One who got you started, Israel: 'Don't be afraid, I've redeemed you. I've called your name. You're mine.'"[16]

By what name does God call us? It is not by all of our given names. It may not even be a name we currently recognize at all. God regularly assigns a new identity to someone when he is preparing them to accomplish great things in His kingdom. Consider these radical business card changes:

- Abram (wealthy business person) became Abraham (father of many nations)[17]
- Simon (catcher of fish for dinner) became Peter (catcher of men for God)[18]
- Saul (murderer of Christians) became Paul (God's greatest evangelist)[19]

---

16 Isaiah 43:1 (MSG)
17 Genesis 17
18 Luke 5
19 Acts 13

The identity re-do I most appreciate is:
- Jacob (fraud, deceiver) became Israel (God-wrestler)[20]

I identify with Jacob's first name and aspire to his second. The Amplified Bible says that when asked his name by God, Jacob in the shock of realization whispers his ashamed reply, "I'm a fraud." God's loving reply is, "Not anymore." God's desire is that we stop scheming and posing behind all of our given names. He blesses us when we wrestle with him all night, refusing to let him go. Only when we embrace our surname of Jesus-follower are we prepared to fully become a member of God's family.

If we choose, we are blessed to inherit the family name of Jesus-follower because of His great sacrifice for us. The beautiful passage from Isaiah 43 quoted earlier goes on to say, "Don't be afraid, I've redeemed you. I've called your name. You're mine. When you're in over your head, I'll be there with you. When you're in rough waters, you will not go down. When you're between a rock and a hard place, it won't be a dead end—Because I am God, your personal God, The Holy of Israel, your Savior. I paid a huge price for you: all of Egypt, with rich Cush and Seba thrown in! That's how much you mean to me! That's how much I love you! I'd sell off the whole world to get you back, trade the creation just for you."[21]

What an amazing thought. God would cash it all in (in fact, he already has) just to allow you and me to inherit the Family name. If God chases so relentlessly after us, shouldn't we persistently pursue others as well? They may come to know him only by our being His children and bearing His name. Given our own

---

20 Genesis 32
21 Isaiah 43:1–4 (MSG)

ancestry, whom are we being called to cozy up to next?

We may not even be aware of this person. We may suffer from a sort of spiritual myopia, able only to see ourselves and our own lives while missing completely the people that God places directly in our path on a daily basis. This is why Jesus asks us the next question in an attempt to restore us to the 20:20 spiritual eyesight he intends us to have: *"Do you see this woman?"*

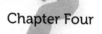

Chapter Four

WHAT IS YOUR NAME?

READ
the following Scripture:
- 1 Kings 18:20–19:18
- Isaiah 43:1–4 (Preferably in *The Message*)

REFLECT
on the following questions:

1. Do you ever choose to remain unknown? Is this in an effort to refresh yourself or to allow you to remain uncommitted or uninvolved?

2. When have you felt isolated like Elijah? What did you do to break out of the darkness? How did God speak to you?

3. What are all of the identities that you carry around?

RESPOND
to the following challenge:

- Take the next 30 days to assess which, if any, of your given names obscure the Royal Identity to which you are called. Commit to praying for how you can fully claim your family name—Jesus-follower—while living out the various roles in your life and work.

Do You See This Woman?

FORGIVENESS

Now one of the Pharisees invited Jesus to have dinner with him, so he went to the Pharisee's house and reclined at the table. When a woman who had lived a sinful life in that town learned that Jesus was eating at the Pharisee's house, she brought an alabaster jar of perfume, and as she stood behind him at his feet weeping, she began to wet his feet with her tears. Then she wiped them with her hair, kissed them and poured perfume on them. When the Pharisee who had invited him saw this, he said to himself, "If this man were a prophet, he would know who is touching him and what kind of woman she is—that she is a sinner."

Jesus answered him, "Simon, I have something to tell you."

"Tell me teacher," he said.

"Two men owed money to a certain moneylender. One owed him five hundred denarii, and the other fifty. Neither of them had the money to pay him back, so he cancelled the debts of both. Now which of them will love him more?"
Simon replied, "I suppose the one who had the bigger debt canceled."
"You have judged correctly," Jesus said. Then he turned toward the woman and said to Simon,

"Do you see this woman?"

Luke 7:36–44

Do You See This Woman?

KURT'S SHOW-STOPPING QUESTION

It was over the top, off the map, crossing...no, obliterating the line. A dancing Elvis in full regalia was gyrating to Las Vegas show tunes to begin church this particular Sunday night. We were not in Kansas anymore, nor in the Lutheran Church of my childhood! You could hear nervous snickering. Tense glances were exchanged with each other. "Is this okay? Will we go to hell for this?"

This was the fourth and final Sunday in a provocative series entitled "God on Location," probing Jesus' teachings on the emotionally charged topics of loss, power and money set against the backdrops of New Orleans, Washington, D.C., and New York. For this evening's teaching, Kurt, the director of the Upper Room Community, had flown with a microphone and John, the intrepid cameraman, to Las Vegas to gather people's 4 a.m. perspectives on love. One after another willing participant brazenly voiced their version of the Las Vegas mantra, "What happens in Vegas, stays in Vegas," as an excuse for all sorts of foolish and reckless behavior. I believed what I was hearing, I just could not quite fathom that I was hearing this saddest of reality shows played out in the confines of our church.

Today, however, it is neither the dancing Elvis nor the sad social commentary on video that still disturbs my soul. It is Kurt's showstopping question summing up Jesus' teaching that Sunday night that continues to haunt me.

It seems there was a prostitute observing all the interviews from a safe distance across the street. As Kurt and John were packing up in the wee hours of the morning, they decided to *cross over to the other side* to gain one more perspective on love—that of the observant prostitute. As they cut across the intersection, she abruptly turned on her stilettos and ran away—in fear, shame, despair, who knows what?

This Epiphany moment caused Kurt to ask, first of himself and then of the assembled Sunday community, "What was it about Jesus that caused prostitutes *not* to run away?" What indeed? Kurt was seeking the perspective—not of liquor-soaked revelers caught on tape, but of the love-soaked Redeemer captured in Scripture—on love and forgiveness.

"Do you see this woman?"[1] In a blinding instant, I saw the prostitute across the street and was abhorred by my corrected vision—not of her, but of myself. I am Simon in the story, questioning Jesus' judgment in my heart, all the while maintaining the front of a religious poser. In truth, until that moment I did not see this woman at all—nor countless other men and women like her. I still miss many of them today. My vision is often clouded by the cataracts of contempt and conceit—lenses on life, hardened by years of judgment. I am forgetful of the forgiveness granted to me for sins neither less nor greater than hers.

Jesus speaks directly and harshly on our judgment of others in His teachings from the hillside in Matthew: "Do not judge, or you too will be judged. For in the same way you judge others, you will be judged, and with the measure you use, it will be measured to you. Why do you look at the speck of sawdust in

---

1   Luke 7:44

your brother's eye and pay no attention to the plank in your own eye? How can you say to your brother, 'Let me take the speck out of your eye,' when all the time there is a plank in your own eye? You hypocrite, first take the plank out of your own eye, and then you will see clearly to remove the speck from your brother's eye."[2] Such a radical correction of vision requires more than mere contact lenses—it requires spiritual LASIK surgery.

Jesus' penetrating question

Jesus slices through layers of pride, contempt and even embarrassment with His penetrating question of vision, "Do you see this woman?"[3] God wastes nothing. His words all carry weight and meaning. His question is laser-focused and Lord-directed. "God means what he says. What he says goes. His powerful Word is sharp as a surgeon's scalpel, cutting through everything, whether doubt or defense, laying us open to listen and obey."[4] We don't read the Bible. The Bible reads us!

Until that instant, Simon likely doubted the prophetic power of Jesus—"If this man was the prophet I thought he was…"—and Simon was surely defensive at having the town whore cause a scene at his house party—"…he would have known what kind of woman this is who is falling all over him."[5] Had he known this was going to happen, Simon would have invited a less prophetic preacher. He was undoubtedly now wishing the woman would vaporize so he could get on with impressing his neighbors.

---

2   Matthew 7:1–5
3   Luke 7:44
4   Hebrews 4:12 (MSG)
5   Luke 7:39 (MSG)

Whether inspired by tepid admiration, false pretenses or celebrity stargazing, an intimate encounter with Jesus always yields more than we ever anticipate. It makes no difference why we seek him—why we invite him to our house for dinner. If invited, Jesus accepts. And it is always an eye-opening experience. He uses the occasion to invert our intentions and radically redirect our life. With Simon, it was the perfect opportunity to teach him (and us) about forgiveness, a lesson I so desperately need to learn and relearn regularly.

SEEING THE INVISIBLE

As part of an annual leadership series I facilitate for county employees, we always tour the facility in which the class is being held. Last year, it was the new city jail. On that particular day, the jail housed 845 people—from men and women just passing through for 24 hours or less to people who would remain there for years.

Our guide attempted to simulate the sequence of events prisoners experience upon arrival at the jail. We began in the bowels of the building, where prisoners entered the facility and proceeded through intake and pat-down, clothing issue, fingerprinting, booking, the "one phone call" booths, mug shot stations and finally to processing. We observed exercise facilities with a basketball hoop and small roof windows to allow tiny shafts of natural light to penetrate the surreal underworld. There were small concrete cells for prisoners who could not coexist with others and cavernous rooms filled with prisoners watching TV, playing cards or reading.

Throughout the tour, I had a growing sense of deep heaviness in my soul. These men and women were, in many cases, the least, the lost and the left out, products of generations of poverty, abuse, neglect and abandonment. It is a vicious cycle of petty crimes to felonious behavior passed on from one generation to the next. The guards knew many of the inmates by both name and pattern of behavior because they had been in prison dozens of times before.

I was relieved that the doors were all locked and that I was visiting for a mere hour. The windows had thick shatterproof glass so I could not hear the thoughts of my imprisoned brothers and sisters. It made it somehow easier to file silently past the cells and avert my gaze from the inmates' looks of anger, wonder, hatred, longing, surprise—to not see them as men and women just like me. And yet I felt an overwhelming sense that the line separating them from me was razor-thin. A different circumstance, choice, upbringing, mentor, spouse, or day—and I could easily have been one of them. There, but by the grace of God, go I.

When we returned to the classroom, I inquired of the 25 somber students, "How do you feel?" One woman's answer reflected my own emotion, "Disoriented."

I had not only lost my sense of direction while walking in circles for one hour in the eight-story windowless prison, I had also become aware of my own blindness through my encounter with the imprisoned men and women.

It is easy to slide past prisoners in jail, never having found ourselves behind bars; to glide past prostitutes on street corners, never having sold our bodies for cash; to ignore immigrants because we grew up here; or to disassociate with the elderly because we still feel young. But then we encounter Jesus.

Jesus always acknowledged the overlooked, loved the unloved
and envisioned the invisible:

- He saw the two sets of brothers, Simon and Andrew[6]
  and James and John,[7] who were bored with their job but
  hungered for a calling.
- He saw Matthew the tax collector in his booth[8] and
  Zacchaeus the chief tax collector in his tree.[9]
- He saw the woman who had been bleeding for 12 years[10]
  and the woman who had been crippled by a spirit for 18
  years.[11]
- He saw the faith of the men who dropped their friend
  through the roof,[12] and the faith of the widow who dropped
  two coins in the temple basket.[13]
- He saw his disciples straining at the oars because of the
  wind[14] and the rich young man straining at life because of
  his wealth.[15]

The perfect setting for Jesus to display His divine field of vision
in Luke's account features the town whore. She was "a woman
who had lived a sinful life in that town."[16] The cast of characters
was all there: a snobby, self-righteous host; a room full of blind
spectators; and a known outcast, a sinner right from their
midst. What is disturbing is that we can see ourselves in every

---

6   Matthew 4:18
7   Matthew 4:21
8   Matthew 9:9; Luke 5:27
9   Luke 19:5
10 Matthew 9:22
11 Luke 13:11
12 Mark 2:5
13 Mark 12:42
14 Mark 6:48
15 Mark 10:21
16 Luke 7:37

cast member. The prostitute's lifestyle had escaped no one, certainly not Simon, whose revulsion of her was expressed in the judgment of his thoughts: "If this man [Jesus] was the prophet I thought he was, he would have known what kind of woman this is who is falling all over him."[17] The implication is that had he this insight, Jesus would have silently glided by the window-less cell imprisoning this promiscuous woman without reaching out or meeting her gaze.

Unlike Simon, however, the prostitute was graced with 20:20 vision. She timidly approached Jesus and "stood behind him at his feet"[18] because she was too humiliated or fearful to look him in the eye. She was not silently sniffling or cautiously crying. The baggage of her brokenness caused her to sob profusely, "raining tears on his feet."[19] She let down her hair, "an act of the gravest immodesty. On her wedding day, a Jewish woman bound up her hair and never would she appear with it unbound again. The fact that this woman loosened her long hair in public showed how she had forgotten everyone—except Jesus."[20] She could not even utter a confession, but thank God at that moment "the Spirit himself intercedes for us with groans that words cannot express."[21]

Only when we pony up to our own pathetic condition—when we bend broken at Jesus' feet, rain tears of remorse, and let down our hair—will we begin to envision our own desperate need for forgiveness. Now we are finally prepared to answer His question.

---

17 Luke 7:39 (MSG)
18 Luke 7:38
19 Luke 7:38 (MSG)
20 William Barclay, *The Gospel of Luke*, 113
21 Romans 8:26

PENNILESS AND WITHOUT A PLAN

There were 7,039,214 personal bankruptcies filed in 2005. The average age was thirty-eight. Forty-four percent of filers were couples, thirty percent were women filing individually and twenty-six percent were individual men. Two out of three filers had lost a job. Half had experienced a serious health problem.[22] This number is increasing daily in the recession of 2008.

The spiritual reality is that 100% of us have to file for personal bankruptcy with God. Whether married, single or divorced; young, middle-aged or old; healthy or ailing; employed or not. Regardless of our economic worth, we do not have the personal worth to buy our way out of brokenness. We are penniless and without a plan.

Jesus awakens Simon to this truth in His teaching on forgiveness: "Two men were in debt to a banker. One owed five hundred silver pieces, the other fifty. Neither of them could pay up, and so the banker canceled both debts. Which of the two would be more grateful?"[23]

Neither man had the money. That is it, isn't it? We really do not have the cash. We are bankrupt—borrowing, as the saying goes, "against money we do not have, to buy things we do not need, to impress people we do not even like!"

William Cope Moyers recalls the moment recovery began for him: "I folded my arms over my chest, longing for comfort, for peace. I was so sick—so sick and tired of it all. In that moment I realized the hopelessness of my situation, and in a sudden, brief

---

22 Administrative Office, U.S. Courts, from BankruptcyAction.com
23 Luke 7:41–42 (MSG)

flash of clarity, I asked myself, 'Now what?' I stared at the filthy wood floor littered with half-empty beer cans, cigarette butts and used syringes. The answer wasn't here in this room any more. It was all over. I was done."[24]

Like William, we deceive ourselves with excuses, religion, friendships, family, health and good intentions. In the end, though, all of these are worthless—insufficient collateral to purchase freedom from our addiction to sin. We are busted!

God's great missionary, Paul, had to admit to the same bankruptcy: "I've spent a long time in sin's prison. What I don't understand about myself is that I decide one way, but then I act another, doing things I absolutely despise.... I decide not to do bad, but then I do it anyway. My decisions, such as they are, don't result in actions. Something has gone wrong deep within me and gets the better of me every time.... It happens so regularly that it's predictable.... I've tried everything and nothing helps. I'm at the end of my rope. Is there no one who can do anything for me? Isn't that the real question?"[25]

Paul concludes that he is "wretched"—miserable, despicable, contemptible—bankrupt.

One of Satan's favorite schemes is to overwhelm us with the crushing weight of our debt. "When he lies, he speaks his native language, for he is a liar and the father of lies."[26] And a favorite lie is that we are hopeless, that we can never get out of hock.

Looking back, William Cope Moyers now believes "any hope

---

24 William Cope Moyers, *Broken: My Story of Addiction and Redemption*
25 Romans, 7:15, 18–19, 23–24 (MSG)
26 John 8:44

worth experiencing is the hope that follows the loss of hope." It is vital to note that he is not referring to *all* hope, but the *false* hope placed in drugs, alcohol, money, looks, business, fame, friendship—even family or religion. All of these are hopeless at the end of the day to buy us out of the debt we have piled up.

God's native tongue is different, a heart language foreign to some perhaps:

- "No one whose *hope* is in you will ever be put to shame."[27]
- "He will not grow tired or weary, and his understanding no one can fathom. He gives strength to the weary and increases the power of the weak. Even youths grow tired and weary, and young men stumble and fall; but those who *hope* in the Lord will renew their strength. They will soar on wings like eagles; they will run and not grow weary, they will walk and not be faint."[28]
- "Now faith is being sure of what we *hope* for and certain of what we do not see."[29]

What are we hoping for? There is no future in "Buy now—pay later. No money down and zero interest until eternity." The bill will come due. And we will not have more collateral then than we do now. We will still be bankrupt.

Thank God the story does not end here. Jesus finished His story with "... so the banker canceled the debts of both."

---

27 Psalm 25:3
28 Isaiah 40:28–31
29 Hebrews 11:1
Italics added

Amazing Grace

Mark Early graduated with a law degree from William and Mary and was in private practice for fifteen years. For the next ten years, he was a Virginia state senator and then served one term as Attorney General of the Commonwealth of Virginia. Mark described his role as "spending a lot of time figuring out how to put more people in prison and then keep them there longer."

After running unsuccessfully for governor in 2001, he was approached by Chuck Colson to be his successor as CEO of Prison Fellowship Ministries. Mark's initial response was "Why would I invest in prisoners at the mid point of my life? If I invest in anyone, they would be people with resources, with reputations, with a standing in the community. Prisoners have no hope and no future."

But as he read his Bible, Mark began to discover God's upside-down economics. He encountered Moses, a fugitive from justice for killing an Egyptian and then burying his crime in the sand.[30] He met Paul, the man specifically called by Jesus to carry His story beyond the Jewish world,[31] but also a man who today would be tried, convicted and sentenced to prison as a co-conspirator in the murder of Stephen.[32] Mark began to understand that God takes the very people we would throw away—the ones who seemingly have no value—and raises them to be the greatest leaders in His community and kingdom. The worthless become priceless. It is precisely because of what characterizes their past that their present and future is so precious. In February of 2002, Mark Early was appointed

---

30 Exodus 2
31 Acts 9
32 Acts 8:11

President and CEO of Prison Fellowship, a ministry which in its 31st year carries the message of God's hope and forgiveness to inmates in all 50 states and over 115 countries.

Jesus' first miracle was one of compassion for a wine-broke groom who was about to suffer the humiliation of his miscalculation. Jesus' greatest miracle is one of love for all of us who are life-broke, having insufficient collateral to buy our way out of spiritual bankruptcy. Jesus offers up His own life as a full payment for our debt. In one amazing act, he picks up our tab and offers us new life and new hope. "I know what I'm doing. I have it all planned out—plans to take care of you, not abandon you, plans to give you the future you hope for."[33]

So what do we do with all of this? When we are awakened to our blindness and convicted of our bankruptcy, when we catch a hint of the vast sum paid to bust us out of our sin's prison, how do we respond? How do we answer Jesus' question?

The point of Jesus' penetrating question in Luke 7 is one of forgiveness. He wants to soften our lens on life so that we see our brothers and sisters—*all* of our brothers and sisters—with eyes focused by forgiveness.

"Do you see this woman? I came to your home; you provided no water for my feet, but she rained tears on my feet and dried them with her hair. You gave me no greeting, but from the time I arrived she hasn't quit kissing my feet. You provided nothing for freshening up, but she has soothed my feet with perfume. Impressive, isn't it? She was forgiven many, many sins, and so she

---

33 Jeremiah 29:11 (MSG)

is very, very grateful."[34] We, too, have been forgiven many, many sins. Our only response is to be very, very grateful, expressed in loving God and forgiving others.

And how do we love each other? It begins by being Jesus for people. When we are cut off on the freeway, we forgive. When we are victims of gossip, we forgive. The anecdote for angry words is forgiveness. The response to devious business dealings is to forgive again. This is not the economic formula of the world that seeks to repay bad deeds with retribution and retaliation. This is not "I don't get mad. I get even!" This is God's economy, which requires that we *be* Jesus because we *see* Jesus in all of our brothers and sisters. We forgive because we were forgiven.

John Newton's beloved hymn celebrates our new eyesight: "Amazing grace! How sweet the sound that saved a wretch like me. I once was lost, but now am found, was blind, but now I see.[35]

The dictionary defines "blind" as
> blind   1) Sightless 2) Unable or unwilling to perceive or understand 3) *Botany.* Failing to produce fruit[36]

The first two definitions are obvious. The third definition, from the science of botany, also makes perfect spiritual sense. If we are blind to our own brokenness, unwilling to perceive the needs of others, we will be unable to produce the fruits of the Spirit in our own lives.

---

34 Luke 7:44–47 (MSG)
35 "Amazing Grace," John Newton
36 Webster's New World Dictionary, 151

As we are lavished with the gifts that accompany forgiveness, do we seek to unload some of our undeserved gain on others, or do we hoard the benefit for ourselves? This is why Jesus continues to deepen our faith journey with His question intended to unleash godly generosity: *"How many loaves do you have?"*

Chapter Five

DO YOU SEE THIS WOMAN?

READ
the following Scripture:
- Matthew 7:1–5
- Romans 7:15–24 (Preferably in *The Message*)
- Isaiah 40:28–31

REFLECT
on the following questions:
1. When have you had a blinding glimpse of God's forgiveness like Kurt?
2. When have you intentionally averted your eyes from seeing someone else?
3. How have you personally experienced God's native language of *hope*?

RESPOND
to the following challenge:
- Focus the next 30 days on *forgiving*—when cut off on the freeway, when the victim of gossip, when underappreciated, when on the receiving end of a tongue-lashing or the silent treatment—forgive and then observe how God brings forth new fruit in your relationships and in your soul.

How Many Loaves Do You Have?

WEALTH

By this time it was late in the day, so his disciples came to him. "This is a remote place," they said, "and it's already very late. Send the people away so they can go to the surrounding countryside and villages and buy themselves something to eat."

But he answered, "You give them something to eat." They said to him, "That would take eight months of a man's wages! Are we to go and spend that much on bread and give it to them to eat?"

"How many loaves do you have?" he asked.

Mark 6:35–38

How many loaves do you have?

THE THIRD OFFERING

Nathan was our guide, driver and interpreter. He and his wife, Sarah, along with their children, serve as missionaries translating the Bible into the Likoni dialect with the Konkomba people of Ghana, West Africa. On this particular morning, he was giving us a crash course in Ghanaian "church" while swerving his Toyota Land Cruiser through the chaotic streets of Accra choked with people and cars. He instructed us that, unlike a typical church service back home, there would be two offerings instead of one. Knowing that we had exchanged minimal U.S. dollars into Cedis, the local currency, he suggested we consider holding a little back from the first offering in order to be able to contribute to the second.

The service began like any in the States. There was a familiar liturgy, hymns with which I grew up, and an order of service that reminded me of countless other Sundays. The choir, resplendent in crimson robes adorned with gold stoles, sang a beautiful anthem following the pastor's message. The first offering was like any other collection I had experienced—the passing of the plate amongst the rows of people, into which the bills and coins representing some percentage of a weekly wage were deposited. I felt confident contributing a few Cedis, knowing that I had several left in anticipation of the second offering.

Shortly after the plates had been brought to the front of the open-air sanctuary, the choir began what I can best describe as a spiritual mamba. They began to slowly weave their way from the back of the church to the front, gathering people from the pews along the route in a dance celebrating God's goodness. While the first offering was a restrained, five-minute affair, the second was a forty-minute wild celebration of God's blessing with singing, dancing, clapping and rhythmic movement that swept up the whole church into the presence of the Spirit. People came forward with coins and bills. Those with neither offered open hands as a testimony of their willingness to give fully of themselves. I snaked my way forward with the throng, thankful for a few Cedis in my pocket but also feeling the birth of transformation from a lifetime of stinginess into a new understanding of true wealth. The Holy Spirit was just beginning to upend me. Eventually, the service returned to a flow with which I was more accustomed—hymns, prayers and the approaching benediction.

Before I could settle back into the comfort of familiarity, however, there was a rustling in the back of the church as a news crew arrived, equipped with cameras and microphones. My colleagues and I were summoned to the front. As the cameras rolled and microphones extended, we were presented with a $2,000 check with this humble apology, "We're so sorry. This is all we can give. We know it's not much. But when we saw the suffering our brothers and sisters in New Orleans endured following Hurricane Katrina, we suffered too. We entrust you with all we could gather up in these past two weeks to help them out."

This third offering was from a 200-member congregation in the heart of a city with 70% unemployment and manual laborers earning an average of $1 per day in wages.

My heart was pierced. As the presentation unfolded, all I could do was weep. This cut to the very core of my selfishness. While I held back in order to smugly contribute to the second offering, my brothers and sisters in Accra gave—not generously or even sacrificially—but foolishly by the world's standards from wells which held no water and wallets that contained no money. They were boldly living out God's dare, the only one contained in Scripture: "Test me in this and see if I don't open up heaven itself to you and pour out blessings beyond your wildest dreams."[1] Is it any wonder why the Christian Church in this African country is experiencing explosive growth and blessing?

JESUS' TESTING QUESTION

Our two sons were both home from college this summer, perhaps for the last time. Their presence has a huge impact on our grocery bill. At 6' 5", our younger son, Joshua, is like a park bear, scavenging the refrigerator and cupboards for food 24/7. When Carol and I are on our way out to do the weekly (daily!) grocery shopping, we do the verbal inventory with the boys: "Do we still have milk? Lunch meat? Yogurt? Cookies? Bread? Cereal?"

Satan tempts to destroy our faith. Jesus tests to display the level of our trust in the power of His provision. When Jesus asked, "How many loaves do you have?" He was not putting together His shopping list. John's account of the same event says that Jesus "already had in mind what he was going to do."[2] He was testing the disciples' understanding of true godly stewardship.

Whoa! Let me stop right there! STEWARDSHIP. What a repulsive word! Both the word and the concept have earned a bad rap over the past several decades. If churches talk about it at all, they talk about it poorly. It has been dumbed down to mean mere

---

1   Malachi 3:10 (MSG)
2   John 6:6

financial management. Stewardship committees conduct annual stewardship campaigns to drum up support for church budgets and programs. Just the word *campaign* should be our first hint that we are way off track. Following Jesus is never a campaign. It is always a conspiracy, with Jesus as the principal conspirator!

"Stewardship is God's way of raising people, not man's way of raising money. God's ways are often about challenging and reshaping our values, our world view. Fundamentally in life, we don't do what we believe. We do what we value."[3]

By asking His testing question, Jesus was zeroing in directly on what His disciples valued. He was making public what most prefer to leave private. But then, he is the God of incisive inquiry. He is asking a question that we must answer.

Jesus did not shy away from the topics of money, possessions, wealth or stewardship. In fact, he taught more on this subject than any other, except the kingdom of God.

Why? Was it because he was addressing wealthy suburbanites who had a lot to manage? Hardly! The followers most drawn to Jesus were among the poorest people in the peasant class. They were unemployed and unemployable. Many were the beggars and outcasts.

Was it because he needed to raise funds to support a staff and building campaign? Surely not. The disciples were unpaid volunteers and Jesus was nomadic, journeying from town to town to live out His calling. "Foxes have holes and birds of the air have nests, but the Son of Man has no place to lay his head."[4]

---

3   Wesley K. Willmer, *Giving to Religion in the 21ˢᵗ Century*
4   Luke 9:58

Jesus spoke openly and often about wealth because he knew that possessions pose a problem. How we deal with what we have tells a deep and consequential story about us. It reveals the condition of our heart and the depth of our trust.

Jesus knew that when he asked, "How many loaves do you have?" the disciples' response would disclose their lack of faith in His unlimited capacity to accomplish His work. It created for them (and for us) a teachable moment, revealing that our hidden desire to withhold, even a few crumbs and sardines, is our biggest deterrent to realizing true wealth. This is a question that he cannot and will not answer for us.

It is crucial to note that the miracle of the feeding of the 5,000 is the only one, other than Jesus' resurrection, to appear in all four Gospels. This story presents the essential truth of what it means to follow Jesus. If we get the answer to Jesus' testing question right in our heart, the tumblers of many other life questions begin to click into place.

What about you?

Are you, like the disciples, feeling the pinch of self-imposed scarcity? Not the true poverty of not having enough, but the gnawing neediness of always wanting a little more. Are you incredulous that Jesus would request giving that goes well beyond generous or even sacrificial to outright foolishness? Do you often feel yourself holding back—giving in to the worldly guidance of "pay yourself first?"

I am with you in all of these. I cannot tell you how many times I sang the old hymn "Take My Life and Let It Be" growing up.

The fourth verse reads, "Take my silver and my gold, not a mite would I withhold."[5] What I *can* tell you is how many times I have actually lived this verse. It would not take both hands to add it up!

So let us journey together as Jesus reverses our feeble interpretation of stewardship. He alone is able to flip our scarcity-minded withholding to a rich understanding of true wealth. The result will be a new abundance of spirit that gives not from what is left but to Who is first.

Selfish Withholding

From the day we were married, Carol and I have comingled our funds. We have joint checking and savings accounts. Our only individual savings are for retirement and a checking account I use to pay business expenses.

Carol is our money manager, not out of desire but out of necessity. It is just not my sweet spot. This became immediately clear when the initial statement from our joint checking account arrived in the first month of our marriage. I gave it a cursory glance and quickly tossed it into the garbage. Carol, with a look of stunned horror, dove headfirst into the can after it. "What are you doing?" was her incredulous question. My off-hand response was, "The same thing I've done with my own statements for years. If we're out of money, the bank will let us know." My days of managing the family finances were finished!

I do not reveal this with great pride or as a best practice for managing financial tension in a relationship. There are plenty of

5   Frances Ridley Havergal, "Take My Life and Let It Be"

good reasons why you might choose a different strategy. Carol and I still have a great deal of emotion fueled by money matters even after nearly thirty years of marriage. The point is that we stumbled early on into the truth that transparency and honesty, particularly in money matters, helps dissipate a lot of stress in a relationship. Withholding is destructive.

It is just this dynamic that Jesus reveals with His miraculous meal. There are three possible explanations of how five loaves and two fish satisfied such a large gathering. The first is that it was a simple matter of multiplication. Jesus summoned His power and exponentially grew five loaves into a bakery and two fish into a hatchery and thousands were fed in one sitting.

A second possibility is that this miracle is really a precursor to Jesus' sacrificial meal in His last days. It powerfully foreshadows the last supper with a prayer of thanksgiving followed by the breaking of bread that nourishes both physically and spiritually.

Both of these explanations are clearly possible. With God, every option is on the table. The third possibility is the most instructive and the most convicting, however. The account in Mark says that when Jesus attempted to move His followers to a remote place for refreshments, word got out and thousands of people went ahead to meet them. While Jesus was sailing across four miles of becalmed water, the crowd was running 10 miles around the top of the lake. Check out the scene that ensues: "There is the crowd; it is late and they are hungry. But was it really likely that the vast majority of that crowd would set out around the lake without any food at all? Would they not take something with them, however little? Now it was evening and they were hungry. *But they were also selfish.*"[6]

---

6   William Barclay, *The Gospel of Mark*, 120–121

The disciples, when encouraged by Jesus to feed the hungry crowd, responded with scoffing, "Are you serious? You want us to go spend a fortune on food for *their* supper?"[7] Their cynical solution was to "Pronounce a benediction and send these folks off so they can get some supper."[8]

And so everybody withheld their food from everybody else, causing the whole body to hunger for both bread and a blessing. The world's wisdom is that what we have is ours. We have earned it. We own it. Our time is ours to spend; our money ours to invest. We have the right to keep it and control it. Save, don't give—especially not to strangers. Where is the return in that?

This is exactly the conventional wisdom that Jesus seeks to radically reverse with His penetrating question. He uses the most unlikely props and the least-willing participants to showcase His path to true wealth.

WEALTHY IN WHAT MATTERS

God wastes nothing. He wants us to internalize every nuance of this miracle because every detail informs how we are to steward wealth as a follower of Jesus. Let us look together and learn from the specifics of the story:

1) *"Here is a boy with five small barley loaves and two small fish, but how far will they go among so many?"*[9]

---

7   Mark 6:37 (MSG), italics added
8   Mark 6:36 (MSG)
9   John 6:9

Barley was the bread of the very poor and was held in contempt because it was often the food offering of a woman caught in adultery. The fish were pickled sardines, likely carried by the boy to help choke down the dry barley bread.

Jesus begins His teaching with a graphic visual of how he can and does work with anything. He is reminding His followers and us that an impoverished adulterer's gift, when put to Royal use in the service of others, is immeasurably more valuable than anything we might squirrel away, no matter how fast, shiny, sexy, expensive or large. Five puny rolls and two pickled fish are the core of an upside-down understanding of stewardship as a Jesus-follower.

2) *"Jesus got them all to sit in groups of fifty or a hundred—
they looked like a patchwork quilt of wildflowers spread out on
the green grass!"*[10]
Church is always community. I love how the Lord's Supper is celebrated at Park Avenue Church in South Minneapolis. The people of that community gather on both sides of the rail in front of the church, shoulder to shoulder, facing each other as they receive the bread and wine. You cannot help but *see* each other, *smell* each other, *feel* each other. It is an intimate meal shared by members of the same family.

Choreographed choirs have distracted us, big-screen power points, orderly 1-hour worship, massive weekend conferences and megachurch madness. The body Jesus was awakening was a ragtag collection of selfish losers that he grouped shoulder to shoulder in fifties and hundreds. They began to break into their own bread because the Bread of Life inspired them with barley loaves and fish from a small boy.

---

10 Mark 6:39 (MSG)

Eugene Peterson's vivid portrayal of the community as a patchwork quilt of wildflowers is wonderfully reminiscent of Jesus' teaching on worry and generosity from His Sermon on the Mount. "Instead of looking at the fashions, walk out into the fields and look at the wildflowers. They never primp or shop, but have you ever seen color and design quite like it? The ten best-dressed men and women in the country look shabby alongside them."[11] The largest, most well-orchestrated mega church service looks pretty shabby next to a community of fifty fully committed to sharing barley loaves with each other, too!

3) *"Taking the five loaves and the two fish and looking up to heaven, he gave thanks and broke the loaves."*[12]
Jesus, who was present when everything was created—"Everything was created through him; nothing—not one thing!—came into being without him."[13]—still has an acute appreciation that everything is God's and therefore gave thanks for the gifts of mere barley loaves and sardines. To forget the creator and owner of everything is ungrateful arrogance.

It is like Donald Miller's friend raking him over the coals when he was complaining he did not have enough money while at the same time admitting to giving very little away: "That is not your money. That is God's money. You ought to be ashamed of yourself stealing from God and all. You write Christian books and everything, and you're not even giving God's money back to him."[14]

---

11 Matthew 6:28–29 (MSG)
12 Mark 6:41
13 John 1:3 (MSG)
14 Donald Miller, *Blue Like Jazz*, 195

Jesus was practicing the teaching of Deuteronomy: "Make sure that when you eat and are satisfied, build pleasant houses and settle in, see your herds and flocks flourish and more and more money come in, watch your standard of living going up and up—make sure you don't become so full of yourself and your things that you forget God, your God."[15]

Moving toward a radical understanding of stewardship begins with the realization that God desires to use everything and everybody, working together in selfless community, fueled by thanksgiving.

4) *"Then he gave them to his disciples to set before the people."*[16] Participants at the National Prayer Breakfast are greeted each year with a little pamphlet entitled *The Strategy of Jesus*, which contains these words from Elton Trueblood's 1947 lecture, *A Radical Experiment:*

"Jesus was deeply concerned for the continuation of His redemptive, reconciling work after the close of His earthly existence, and His chosen method was the formation of a small band of committed friends. He did not form an army, establish a headquarters, or even write a book. What he did was to collect a very few common men and women, inspire them with the sense of His spirit and vision, and build their lives into an intensive fellowship of affection, worship and work.

One of the truly shocking passages of the Gospel is that in which Jesus indicates that there is absolutely no substitute for the tiny, loving, caring, reconciling society. If this fails, he suggests, all is failure; there is no other way. He told the little bedraggled

---

15 Deuteronomy 8:12–14 (MSG)

16 Mark 6:41

fellowship that they were actually the salt of the earth, and that if this salt should fail there would be no adequate preservative at all. He was staking it all on one throw."[17]

With the crushing volume of need in the world today, we are God's plan. He always works through people. He must. God has no "Plan B." He gives us the bread and fish and then waits to see whether we distribute it or stuff it deep into our own pockets. We must answer His question with our actions.

5) *They all ate and were satisfied, and the disciples picked up twelve basketfuls of broken pieces of bread and fish."*[18]

The result of true wealth is *contentment*. Now there is a word seldom spoken. When was the last time you uttered the words *satisfied* or *content* in conversation? The very concept has taken on the negative connotation of being a slacker.

There were 12 basketfuls of fish and chips, one for each of the reluctant disciples, left over as a testimony of God's power to fully satisfy. Paul writes of this supernatural satisfaction in his letter to the Philippian believers: "I know what it is to be in need, and I know what it is to have plenty. I have learned the secret of being content in any and every situation, whether well fed or hungry, whether living in plenty or in want."[19]

Do you want "the secret"? I do! Forget the current bestselling book by the same title. Paul had it scooped centuries ago! The secret is "I can do everything through him who gives me strength."[20]

---

17 Elton Trueblood, *A Radical Experiment*
18 Mark 6:42–43
19 Philippians 4:12
20 Philippians 4:13

The miracle is not one of mere multiplication. It is the softening of selfish hearts. True wealth, in God's upside-down world, is only accomplished through His body of followers giving sacrificially of themselves to others. Only God can reverse our withholding to wealth, our concealment to contentment.

So what shall we do with the 12 baskets of leftovers? It is just this concern that Jesus seeks to address with His next penetrating question, *"Will you give me a drink?"*

Chapter Six

HOW MANY LOAVES DO YOU HAVE?

READ
the following Scripture:
- Mark 6:35–44
- Deuteronomy 8:2–5, 10–20

REFLECT
on the following questions:

1. Where are you currently withholding
your money, time or giftedness?

2. If "God's ways are fundamentally about reshaping our values,
our worldview," how is he currently reshaping yours?

3. Why do you believe Jesus spoke so often
and so openly about money?

RESPOND
to the following challenge:

- Endeavor the next 30 days to be deeply thankful. Start and end each day with an extended time of thanksgiving, for gifts large and small. See how this practice impacts your faith journey and your sense of true wealth.

-or-

- Jesus' strategy was "to collect a very few common men and women, inspire them with a sense of His spirit and vision, and build their lives into an intensive fellowship of affection, worship and work." Do you have such a fellowship? Use the next 30 days to assess your current fellowship, and to increase the intensity level of its affection, worship and/or work.

Will You Give Me a Drink?

GENEROSITY

The Pharisees heard that Jesus was gaining and baptizing more disciples than John, although in fact it was not Jesus who baptized, but his disciples. When the Lord learned of this, he left Judea and went back once more to Galilee.

Now he had to go through Samaria. So he came to a town in Samaria called Sychar, near the plot of ground Jacob had given to his son Joseph. Jacob's well was there, and Jesus, tired as he was from the journey, sat down by the well. It was about the sixth hour.

When a Samaritan woman came to draw water, Jesus said to her,

"Will you give me a drink?"

John 4:1–7

Will You Give Me a Drink?

SANDRA'S CLINCHING QUESTION

Every July our church sponsors a series called Summer Voices. This is an opportunity for people from outside our community to share how God is challenging them as activists and leaders in this season of their life. Sandra was the first to share her heart last summer. She is a part-time pastor at a North St. Paul church and director of The Lift, a nonprofit that works with at-risk students. Several years ago, Sandra and her husband felt called to move from the suburbs into the city to live out their faith in a visceral way.

I must admit that, for the first part of her talk, I was guilty of CPA—continuous partial attention—"uh-huhing" a lot of her experiences and intellectually agreeing with her assertions. My head was in it, but my heart was miles away.

But then Sandra stopped and shared a series of questions that had caused her to do a one-eighty on faith and hunger. "Suppose," she said, "that you were going to buy new curtains for your house and someone next door was starving. Is it OK to still buy the curtains?" *No brainer,* I thought. *Of course not!* "But what if that person lives at the end of the block? Then what?" *Well, I suppose I'd pitch in,* I thought. "What about just in the neighborhood?" Now this was getting tougher. I don't know all the people in my neighborhood. How would I know? Would I care?

"How far away does the person have to be before it's OK to buy curtains and *let them starve to death*?" she asked. Now Sandra had my full attention! Her summer voice had moved out of my head and was reverberating in my heart.

What little we hear about the poor in the U.S. often refers to them as a group, species or statistic from some distant land. In truth, 24,000 people die each day from hunger or hunger-related diseases, one every 3.6 seconds. But they do not die as a class. They perish one at a time—as brothers, sisters, fathers, mothers, daughters, sons—leaving behind heartbroken families attempting to carry on in extreme poverty while coping with deep grief.

Alexandr Solzhenitsyn, in his brilliant Nobel Lecture in Literature from 1970, makes this pointed observation: "We confidently judge the whole world according to our own home values. Which is why we take for the greater, more painful and less bearable disaster, not that which is in fact greater, more painful and less bearable, but that which lies closest to us. Everything which is further away, which does not therefore threaten this very day to invade our threshold—with all its groans, its stifled cries, its destroyed lives, even if it involves millions of victims—this we consider on the whole to be perfectly bearable and of tolerable proportions."[1]

I have become quite accomplished at "bearing." Perhaps it is a defense mechanism so as to not be overwhelmed by the news of typhoons ravaging, earthquakes burying and hurricanes devastating, more often than not, the poor in places that seem distant and remote. I don't dare utter the prayer of Bob Pierce, founder of World Vision and Samaritan's Purse, "Let my heart be broken with the things that break the heart of God." Truthfully, I'm terrified of the consequences of such a request. I tend to cover my eyes and protect my heart from seeing or feeling the hungry, parched or poor.

---

1   Alexandr Solzhenitsyn, Nobel Lecture in Literature (1970)

JESUS' REVEALING QUESTION

Jesus never averted His eyes or heart from the poor or suffering. In fact, throughout Scripture and in the world today, they are God's primary focus. "God is in the slums, in the cardboard boxes where the poor play house. God is in the silence of a mother who has afflicted her child with a virus that will end both of their lives. God is in the cries heard under the rubble of war. God is in the debris of wasted opportunity and lives and God is with us if we are with them."[2]

John's account states that God *had* to go through Samaria. Geographically, this was not true. Palestine, where Jesus was working, was approximately 120 miles from north to south, and consisted of three distinct regions: Galilee in the north, Samaria in the middle, and Judea in the south. The quickest route from Judea back to Galilee was directly through Samaria—a trek of about three days. Because of a bitter racial feud dating back over 7 centuries, Jews would avoid Samaria like the plague and venture along the Jordan River outside Samaria and reenter Palestine in Galilee, thereby doubling the travel time but keeping themselves insulated from the impure Samaritans.

It seemed that Jesus was ducking out of trouble by leaving just as the Pharisees were stirring up conflict among believers by keeping score in the baptism sweepstakes. But then, being the God of great contradictions, Jesus stepped squarely into a far bigger controversy by leading His small band of followers directly through Samaria. To make the story more outrageous, Jesus asked His revealing question of a *Samaritan…woman…*who had been *married 5 times…* and was now living with a *sixth man!*

---

2   Bono, National Prayer Breakfast (February 2006).

Let me break this down a little. First, rather than choosing the respectable and religiously correct route, Jesus strides directly into the home territory of racially impure half-breeds, the Samaritans. There he speaks to a woman at a Jewish landmark spot, Jacob's well. Philip Yancy says that, "In those days, at every synagogue service, Jewish men prayed, 'Blessed art Thou, O Lord, who hast not made me a woman.' Women sat in a separate section, were not counted in quorums, and were rarely taught the Torah. In social life, few women would talk to men outside of their own families, and a woman was to touch no man but her spouse."[3] Jewish Rabbis, in particular, were never to speak to a woman in public, not even their wife, daughter or sister.

As if to put an exclamation point on His scandalous behavior, Jesus speaks to a woman who had been married five times and was now living with a sixth man. This likely explained why she was at Jacob's well, alone and at this hour. There was a well in her town of Sychar, but she chose to walk the half mile to draw water. She was alone rather than with other women of Sychar. She was there in the midday heat rather than at dawn or dusk. The whole setup sighs of shame, loneliness and humiliation. This woman was penniless in possessions and flat-out broke in spirit, living on the fringe of her own village. In other words, she was right in Jesus' sweet spot!

The first person with which Jesus chooses to reveal the secret of His true identity and to ignite a revival in a long-scorned region was this five-times married Samaritan woman. Jesus starts a revolution by asking for *her* help, and in so doing desires to open *our* eyes to the reality of true generosity.

---

3 Philip Yancy, *The Jesus I Never Knew,* 153–154.

What about you? Are you guarding your heart from the ravages of world disasters or from the poor just down the street? Have you become skilled at "bearing"?

Are the cries of today's Samaritan women muffled by miles or diminished by distance? Jesus moves from our heads to our hearts with His question, "Will you give me a drink?" It jars us out of our spiritual lethargy and teaches us that any request for basic needs can be a divine call from God himself to respond generously with mercy, justice and humility. He seeks to turn upside down our narrow focus from getting to giving—even giving the smallest amounts of our most basic gifts. Will we give him a drink? He waits for our answer.

ROLLS ROYCE RELIGION

Running through the Minneapolis airport two years ago, my attention was grabbed by the *Time* magazine on the newsstand display. "Does God Want You to be Rich?" asked the lead story. The provocative cover art featured the grill of a Rolls Royce with a cross as the hood ornament. The article was a description of the new gospel of wealth—also dubbed the "prosperity gospel" or "name-it-and-claim-it theology." Of Christians surveyed, 17% said they considered themselves part of this movement and 61% believed that God wants people to be prosperous. Unfortunately, 31% concluded that if you give your money to God, he would bless you with more money.[4]

This belief system is especially seductive as the world's economy heads south. Lear-jetting telepreachers paint Jesus as a sort of

---

4 *Time,* (September 18, 2006), 50.

blessed byway to the 5 Cs: clothes, cars, cash, clubs and credit. Philosophically, their way of helping the poor is to "encourage people not to be one of them."[5]

The lure of this message turns former NBA arenas into megachurches and sells millions of books. This is all very interesting, but antithetical to Jesus' point of view and call to action.

When Jesus delivered His first temple talk back in His hometown of Nazareth, he announced the mission for His entire ministry. It was clearly not a message of today's "name-it and claim-it" theology! He names the focal point for His blessing—"God's Spirit is on me; he's chosen me to preach the Message of good news to *the poor*, Sent me to announce pardon to *prisoners* and recovery of sight to the *blind*, To set the *burdened and battered* free…"[6] And His claim is one of action, right here and right now—"*This* is God's year to act!"[7] Jesus' message was so well received that His own townspeople tried to throw Him off a cliff! A similar message today may net the same result. We desire a softer message aimed at a more sanitized crowd. We would rather shield our eyes from the poor, continue to lock up the imprisoned, patronize the blind and say a prayer for the burdened and battered. But really act? Not so much! The claims I stake are often for my own interests, praying for more blessings to be heaped on an already abundantly blessed life. This is not the generosity of which Jesus speaks.

Jesus was quoting from Isaiah 61 when he stated His ministry's purpose. This chapter in the Bible follows closely behind one

---

5   *Time,* (September 18, 2006), 55.
6   Luke 4:18 (MSG), italics added.
7   Luke 4:19 (MSG), italics added.

of the clearest descriptions of godly generosity. Isaiah 58 is titled "True Fasting" in most translations, but it is also a perfect account of the unselfishness that only God can inspire. "This is the kind of fast day (generosity) I'm after: to break the chains of injustice, get rid of exploitation in the workplace, free the oppressed, cancel debts. What I'm interested in seeing you do is: sharing your food with the hungry, inviting the homeless poor into your homes, putting clothes on the shivering ill-clad, being available to your own families."[8] This vivid portrait is easy to envision but very demanding to practice.

The best way to learn is to teach—and the most powerful way to teach is to embody the message in bold actions, not mere words. I would rather see a sermon than hear one any day.

BOB'S SLEEP OUT

Thirteen years ago, the owner of a small shoe repair shop named Bob Fisher began living out a sermon for the working poor and marginalized people in his community. In a moment of questionable sanity, he decided to take up winter camping in Minnesota! His first outing in his backyard taught him that even a sleeping bag rated to plus 20 degrees offered slim protection against a cold, early winter evening. But while he was breathing the polar air inside his pup tent, God breathed into Bob a powerful vision, challenging him to "share in His sufferings."[9] God weeps when His people suffer, so he was inviting Bob to weep with him for the poor of Wayzata, Minnesota.

In November 1996, Bob committed to sleeping out in his

---

8   Isaiah 58:6–7 (MSG)
9   Philippians 3:10

tent until he raised $7,000 to buy Thanksgiving dinners for 100 families. In 14 days, Bob was back in his warm bed with $10,000 collected for meals. But his journey of obedience to God's invitation had just begun. A local ministry, Interfaith Outreach and Community Partners, challenged Bob to sleep out again the next year for the working poor and homeless. Thus was born "Bob's Sleep Out." It quickly morphed from one cobbler's mission to a whole community-wide commitment to the Samaritan women of this largely affluent suburb of Minneapolis. Since 1996, 3,000 community members including churches, businesses, youth and civic groups have raised over $10.5 million to provide shelter for the homeless.

One of my favorite photos of our son Josh was taken when he supported the Sleep Out his junior year in high school. Bob showed up at midnight, in driving rain in the middle of a goose poop-infested football field, to encourage Josh and all of his classmates as they lived their faith out loud. The picture shows Bob with 50 wide-eyed, wet and cold high school students hanging on his every word. For them, he was "Jesus with skin on" that evening in front of their tents. If he were merely preaching a sermon, they would have crawled back into the relative warmth of their sleeping bags. But a sermon lived out in selfless actions, now that was worthy of time spent standing out in the cold and rain!

Do not let Bob's story intimidate you into inaction. Many acts of generosity are a smaller response to the most basic needs of the poor and hungry. The cumulative effect of thousands of small, individual actions have the power to make a vast difference.

ZIPPERS FOR JESUS

Several years ago I was running out of the office, late as usual, to catch a flight. "Do you want any money?" Susan asked, as I sprinted past her desk. *Who doesn't?* I thought.

It turned out that we had sold a large number of books at a conference the evening before, and Susan was sitting on a pile of cash. She was offering to unload some of it on me rather than take it all to the bank. Impulsively I replied, "I'll take all you've got!" I stuffed $750 in small bills into my roll aboard and scrambled off to the airport. Only when I was walking through the scanners at the terminal did it occur to me that I looked like a drug runner!

I had the wild idea of giving the money away to participants in a *STEWARDshift™* program that I was facilitating the next day in Seattle. That evening, I sat on the bed in my hotel room and sorted the money into 100 envelopes, each containing between $2 and $60. The following day, I challenged each participant to follow a certain rhythm with the money and see how God responded as a result. God blesses each of us. Some get a little, some get much more. Regardless of what they received, each participant was to *pray* for God's guidance, *give* the money away, *watch* where it went and, if they were willing, *share* the outcome of their generosity. The only nonnegotiable was that they had to give it all away. They could not keep the cash. The task was simply to follow God's Isaiah 58 directive—in other words, to take God at His word. This was honestly the best idea I had all year!

One of the recipients of the envelopes was Pastor Jack. He in turn added some of his own money, subdivided it into 12 new envelopes and passed them along with the same instructions to his confirmation class: *pray, give, watch* and *share*. Several weeks later, he sent their initial reaction via e-mail, "The group was far more quiet and serious than usual. I outlined the *pray-give-watch-share* plan with them. We paused in quiet prayer…asking for discernment on how to be a faithful conduit of whatever was in the envelope. Then, as each opened theirs, no one was disappointed or giddy as I really think the prayer beforehand made them realize this was theirs to give—not keep. One of the rougher but lovable guys told the others, 'Remember, God and Pastor Jack will be pissed if we pocket it for ourselves!' Success!!"

What did these empowered ninth graders do with the money in order to not "piss off" God or Pastor Jack? Two guys pooled their $27, bought ten pounds of sliced turkey and ham, a jar of peanut butter, some jelly and loaves of bread and made "a mess of sandwiches" for the Gospel Mission's Men's and Women's Shelters. One girl used her $5 for a new zipper to repair an unused coat and donated it to a local clothing drive. Another girl bought $11 worth of Taco Bell certificates to hand out to the frequent panhandlers on the interstate exit ramps. Three others went to make toy purchases for the Marines Toys for Tots drive. Each of these cool ninth graders heard the call of the poor for basic needs and answered with simple but profound creativity and compassion.

GIVING AND GETTING

God promises to reward such generosity with a series of powerful outcomes in Isaiah 58: "Do this and the lights will turn on, and your lives will turn around at once. Your righteousness will pave your way. The God of glory will secure your passage. *Then when you pray, God will answer. You'll call out for help and I'll say, 'Here I am.'* I will show you where to go. I'll give you a full life in the emptiest of places—firm muscles, strong bones. You'll be like a well-watered garden, a gurgling stream that never runs dry."[10] If we want to hear God's voice, we need only hear the poor. If we want to be spiritually well hydrated, we must attend to the parched interstate panhandlers. If we want the lights to stay on in our house, we need to keep the lights on for the homeless.

God does not mandate a tithe of time or money. He is not into grudge giving—feeling forced to give, or greed giving—giving in order to get. He desires that we move from "serve-*us*" to "service." The gift he requires is for us "to act justly to love mercy and to walk humbly,"[11] especially with people on the margins. Rather than pervert the Gospel into a cheesy "give-to-get scheme," Jesus reveals the outcome of true godly generosity in His unlikely interaction with the Samaritan woman. She did not give the casual or the costless. She gave it all.

As a result of His inquiry, the woman runs to her village and brings all of her judgmental townies out to meet Jesus. The poor Samaritan woman becomes a powerful missionary, igniting a revival in a long-scorned land. Jesus stays on two more days with the Samaritans at their invitation, harvesting the rewards of the lonely woman's gift of water for a weary Rabbi.

Just as with the Samaritan woman, Jesus asks us for *our* help today. Through our actions, the poor are fed, the naked clothed and the prisoners set free. What do we get in return? We are freed from our own slavery to selfishness and can fully

---

10   Isaiah 58:8–9, 11 (MSG), italics added.

11   Micah 6:8

experience the pure joy of a ninth grader's gift of a zippered coat. Jesus offers us living water that does not run dry and spiritual food that never ceases to satisfy. Through our generosity, we become like a well-watered garden to which others are drawn for nourishment and survival.

To give is more blessed than to receive. Actually, it is *only* in giving that we truly receive the best stuff! Jesus seeks to check our level of commitment to others and to him with His last, most important question, *"Do you truly love me?"*

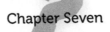

Chapter Seven

WILL YOU GIVE ME A DRINK?

READ
the following Scripture:
- Isaiah 58:1–14
- Philippians 3:8–10

REFLECT
on the following questions:

1. Rather than "bearing," what current world events are breaking your heart because they are breaking the heart of God?

2. What is your answer to *Time* magazine's cover story question, "Does God Want You to Be Rich?"

3. Which of the promises in Isaiah 58:8–14 do you find most exhilarating?

RESPOND
to the following challenge:

- Take the same *Pray-Give-Watch-Share* challenge as Pastor Jack's kids with a small group of your friends over the next 30 days, and see where and how God blesses your efforts.

Do You Truly Love Me?

LOVE

When they had finished eating, Jesus said to Simon Peter, "Simon son of John,

Do you truly love me more than these?"

"Yes, Lord," he said, "you know that I love you." Jesus said, "Feed My Lambs."
Again Jesus said, "Simon son of John, do you truly love me?"
He answered, "Yes Lord, you know that I love You." Jesus said, "Take care of my sheep."
The third time he said to him, "Simon son of John, do you love me?" Peter was hurt because Jesus asked him the third time, "Do you love me?" He said, "Lord, you know all things; you know that I love you." Jesus said, "Feed my sheep."

John 21:15–17

Do You Truly Love Me?

APHAM'S LOVING QUESTION

I am blessed to see a miracle almost every other Friday. My friend Keith is a study in physical and personal contrasts. On the one hand, he is a mountain of a man, standing 6' 7" tall with striking features and huge, gnarled hands. At the same time, his imposing body is breaking down bit by bit, the result of fourteen years spent in the trenches of professional football. Keith anchored the offensive line in two Super Bowl victories and faced the violent rush of defensive linemen bent on destroying Joe Montana. But his spirit is as soft and transparent as any man I know. His heart melts at the requests of his wife and three daughters. He stood in the arena where many men only dream of playing, yet speaks of it only when asked. Keith is a humble warrior. For all of these reasons and many more, he has become one of my dearest friends over the last fifteen years.

One Friday six years ago, Keith revealed to our Friday guy's group that he was dying. He had suffered from polycystic kidney disease all of his life. But now his tumor-choked kidneys were slowly shutting down. Keith had submitted his name for organ donation, but the wait for receipt of a cadaver kidney averaged over four years. He was beginning to fear that he did not have that long to live, but was trying to avoid the painful daily routine of dialysis so as to preserve the integrity of his kidneys. His condition was deteriorating rapidly.

"Coincidentally," on this same Friday, Apham was visiting our group for the first time. He had been invited by one of our regular attendees to describe his passion for starting a Christian radio station in his native country of Nigeria. He happened to be there the morning that Keith described his failing health. While interesting to Apham, much of Keith's plight fell on deaf ears. After all, he did not know this big guy. And, just a few years earlier, Apham had vigorously argued with his wife Janel about organ donation. When she had renewed her driver's license, Janel had indicated her desire to donate her organs in the event of death. Apham's strongly held view was that if she passed away in some tragic accident, "she would be going to meet God with all of her organs intact!"

Our group requested that Apham report back following his exploratory trip to Nigeria to assess the viability of starting a radio station. While in Nigeria, one of the many experiences that God provided him was an encounter with a woman hoping to generate pity by using her dying child to beg for food. Try as hard as he could, Apham could not blot out the memory of Keith's condition from his mind. It was as if God kept snapping Keith back into his heart's focus through the lives and circumstances Apham encountered almost daily.

When Apham returned to our group several weeks later, Keith was absent. His question, "Where's the big guy?" was met with a sober update. Most nights Keith would lie shivering in bed, unable to get warm, even when wrapped in a down coat and comforter. His deterioration was accelerating. Apham was the fifth man in our group of twelve to inquire about donating a kidney to Keith. What makes this remarkable was that Apham's loving question was on the basis of his very first encounter with Keith. The story moves from remarkable to miraculous when you consider that Apham, a life-long Oakland Raiders fan, was offering to donate his kidney to Keith, who played his entire career for the archrival San Francisco 49ers! God's love really does conquer all!

Fast-forward to a gloomy February Sunday two months later. After slogging two blocks through the snow and sleet from our parked car, Carol and I ran into Apham and his family as we entered church. His answer to my benign "What's up?" was stunning. "Well," he said, "I lost my job, and this week I donate my kidney to Keith!"

What are the chances that a Nigerian man, in the U.S. for only ten years, would be a *perfect match* for a native Minnesotan, fifteen years his elder, from little St. Cloud? The only thing that they had in common was a shared passion for American football—and their faith. That qualifies as a "God thing"! Only God could have been orchestrating this miraculous connection for decades. But Apham still had to say "Yes!" to God's question, "Do you truly love me?" He needed to pay attention to all of the markers God was putting in his path. Like Apham, we too must answer this pivotal question for ourselves.

JESUS' PIERCING 3-FOLD QUESTION

Jesus confronted Peter, His most impulsive follower, with a piercing question of love shortly after His resurrection. Jesus' closest followers had returned almost immediately to their former profession following His death. Just three years earlier, Jesus had challenged them to put down their nets and take up His calling, becoming "fishers of men."[1] But now, having watched their leader suffer a brutal and inglorious death, they must have been wondering if they had just spent the previous three years betting on the wrong horse.

---

1 Matthew 4:19

Many people have experienced the crushing defeat of disillusionment. Pastors of large churches have been exposed as frequent practitioners of the very moral failure they condemn every Sunday morning. Investment gurus have made off with the life savings of trusting investors. Business leaders have traded away whole companies of multigenerational employees in the name of progress and innovation. But the followers of Jesus had the added burden of believing that he was the Promised One. They had staked their whole life and livelihood on following Jesus, and now it seemed they were left out in the cold.

Only days earlier, Peter had pledged his allegiance to Jesus— "Master, I'm ready for anything with you. I'd go to jail for you. I'd die for you!"[2] This was Peter's style. Peter is not like John, who "leaned back against Jesus"[3] Peter was a "talk first, think later" guy. He was regularly guilty of making brash statements and bold predictions. He lived his adoration of Jesus fully out loud. Peter is the patron saint of ADHD Jesus-followers! Shortly after his bold claim, however, Peter had denied even knowing Jesus to save his own skin. Now, with hopes dashed and only the bitter memory of recent failure, Peter was sitting in his skivvies in the middle of the lake soaking worms. Adding insult to injury, it appeared that the three-year layoff from fishing had diminished his skill. He had spent the whole evening with friends getting totally skunked!

It is into this setting that Jesus inserts himself, demonstrating for all time that he has real power over death and evil. He shows up not as some ethereal vapor, but as a real person, cooking over a campfire. Jesus serves up a shore breakfast to his disillusioned disciples, proving once again that he is attentive not only to our

---

2 Luke 22:33 (MSG)
3 John 21:20

spiritual needs, but also to our most basic physical requirements. It is at this inaugural prayer breakfast that he asks Peter what appears to be the same question three different times.

Jesus is not assuming that Peter or we are slow of head or hard of heart. He is asking three distinct questions, all aimed at clarifying the intensity of our love for him. Do we truly love him, *more than these* other things that would dim our devotion? Do *we* truly love him, enough to ultimately trust His undying desire for us? Do we *love* him, not like friends or family, but with unrestrained passion and purpose? Each of these questions is at the very essence of our journey of faith. Our answers define the focus of our faith and the enjoyment of our existence. Jesus asks, but we must answer His crucial 3-fold question of love.

Gaining a perfect perspective

I experience the tagline of the movie *The Sixth Sense* almost every time I step into a crowded elevator in an office building or corporate headquarters: "I see dead people!" People are numbed from the heart up by the incessant Muzak of memos and busy-ness of business. The illusion of technology as the ticket to a more leisurely life has given way to the reality of a 24/7 world of connectivity. A friend recently confided that he believes "technology is the new idolatry." He was basing this on his observation of a person going forward in church to receive Holy Communion while working his Blackberry! The pretense that because we are *so* important, we must remain tethered at all times, and at any cost to our office, colleagues and friends, is choking our human spirit. We know intuitively that "more"—business, friendships, possessions—is not a promise but a promissory note that will ultimately demand our health, relationships, faith or even our life as payment. Yet we press on, surreptitiously doing the "Blackberry prayer" whenever we can sneak it in.

The Reset button is currently being pressed worldwide. After years of gravity-defying portfolios and housing prices, insane work hours, and an endless upward arc of career and personal aspirations, all in the interest of moving up or moving on, the bill is being presented in the form of a global recession. Our hurry sickness has given way to real illness. Years of "cup-holder cuisine" have resulted in bloated bodies and significance-starved souls.

Jesus sweeps His hand over this whole scene and asks, "Do you truly love me *more than these?*"[4] What is Jesus really asking of Peter and us? Perhaps he was referring to the large haul of fish and is questioning whether we are prepared to loosen our dependence on all of our false securities, including work, in order to fully grasp a total reliance on him. Jesus was calling out Peter and his buddies on their rapid retreat to the comforts of their former job. Apham was laid off right before his kidney donation, freeing him to answer God's question posed through Keith with a resounding "Yes!" The man by the pool in Chapter 3 set down his vocation of begging in order to pick up his calling to heal others. The Samaritan woman at the well in Chapter 7 put aside her daily work of fetching water in order to gather up followers of Jesus. What must we let go of?

Jesus is seeking to place our priorities in perspective. Everything—work, relationships, health, finances—when placed in the queue behind our devotion to God, finds new purpose and meaning. Even our service of God needs to step into line.

4 John 21:15, italics added

Dallas Willard suggests, "The greatest enemy of intimacy *with God* is service *to God*."

It seems paradoxical, but the biggest danger we face is not sin. It is busy-ness, especially for God's sake.

I was always moved by the throng of people stepping forward at the conclusion of every Billy Graham Crusade. They came from the upper decks and bleacher seats, responding to the message, and moving with the stanzas of the old hymn, "Just As I Am." The legitimate rap, however, is that far too often we sing *Just As I Am,* we come *just as we are,* but we live *just as we were!* We are being challenged in Jesus' question to reprioritize our lives in favor of never again living *just as we were.* Peter's bold response was, "Yes, Master, you know I love you (more than these fish)."[5] He put down, once and forever, fishing for mere fish.

Are our priorities in order? Would our response to Jesus' question be the same? What needs to step to the back of the procession in order for us to leap boldly across the portal and become a fully devoted follower of Jesus like Peter?

MET BY JEFF AT THE PEARLY GATES

One of the truly precious verses in the Bible is Mark 16:7. An angel tells three women who sought to anoint Jesus' dead body in the grave to run and get His followers together for a joyous reunion. "But go, tell his disciples *and Peter,* 'He is going ahead of you into Galilee. There you will see him, just as he told you.'"[6] *And Peter!* Those two little words say it all. Jesus wanted especially to

---

5 John 21:15 (MSG), parentheses added
6 Mark 16:7, italics added

reconnect with Peter after his three-fold denial in the courtyard. He wanted to reassure Peter that no one has sinned so greatly so as to disqualify them from God's grace.

How do you picture heaven? Is your heaven a place of luxurious scenery and eternal respite from the worries of this life? Do you envision it like the beginning of many old and tired jokes, "So a guy dies and goes to heaven. There, he's met at the pearly gates by St. Peter, and..." My grandfather wrote a beautiful little book on heaven, inspired in part by his experience of ministering to Lester Kahl, a convicted murderer, just before he was hung. I am sure he was thinking of reuniting with Lester at the pearly gates as he wrote.

Do you ever imagine being met at the pearly gates by Jeffrey Dahmer? I'll bet that question got your attention! Dahmer's name and image is synonymous with "monster." Between 1978 and 1991, he raped, murdered and dismembered 17 young boys and men. He sampled cannibalism with at least one corpse. He stored his victims in vats. As punishment for his heinous crimes, the court imposed 15 consecutive life sentences, thus requiring that Jeffrey Dahmer serve a minimum of 936 years in prison. On November 28, 1994, a fellow inmate killed Dahmer with a single blow to the skull. It would seem that this sickest of stories ended in the Columbia Correctional Institution in Portage, Wisconsin.

But Peter's story did not end with his denial, and Jeffrey Dahmer's story did not end with his incarceration. Six months before his death, Dahmer was baptized by immersion in a whirlpool tub by Roy Ratcliff, a local minister. After his conversion, Dahmer began meeting on a weekly basis to pray and study Scripture. Now he joins the ranks of other murders in heaven such as the apostle Paul, Moses and King David. I would say he is keeping pretty good company!

The fourth-century biblical scholar Jerome offers an explanation for the specificity of John's account. Why does it matter that John enumerates 153 fish in the net? Jerome suggests "that in the sea, there are 153 different kinds of fish: and that the catch is one which includes every kind of fish: and that therefore the number symbolizes the fact that someday *all* people of *all* nations will be gathered together in Christ." Furthermore, "this great catch of fishes was gathered into the net, and the net held them all and was not broken. The net stands for the church: and there is room in the church for *all* people of *all* nations."[7] There is even room for Peter—and for Jeffrey Dahmer.

In asking the question, "Do *you* truly love me?" Jesus is checking whether we *really* believe that all people are so precious in His sight that we are willing to put down our prejudices and preconceptions. The most judgmental question many Christians ask is, "But is that person a believer?" The response I have recently adopted is "Only God knows!" I am not trying to be flippant or rude. I am being honest. He asks Peter, "Do *you* truly love me?" He does not ask, "Do you think John loves me? What about James? And Thomas—that dude sure has some doubts! As a matter of fact, I think from now on I will label him 'doubting Thomas'!" No, he asks Peter for *his* personal commitment. He desires the same from each of us. Do *we* truly love him?

I recently read the percentage of Americans who have never known:
- a Buddhist – 59 percent
- an undocumented immigrant – 54 percent
- a Muslim – 46 percent
- a homeless person – 45 percent

---

7 William Barclay, *The Gospel of John,* 331, italics added

- an evangelical Christian – 40 percent
- a political liberal – 25 percent
- a political conservative – 24 percent
- a former inmate – 15 percent
- a wealthy person – 12 percent[8]

Given our ignorance of others, we had better speak only for ourselves. Jesus asks, "Do *you* truly love me?" Do we trust that the net will not break, no matter the size and scope of His catch? Can we lay aside believing that we know which varieties of fish are considered a "good catch?"

UNCONDITIONAL LOVE

Words matter. The depth of our understanding of Jesus' third piercing question is determined by our grasp of the language of love. "Love" has many meanings in the English language, and has been cheapened by tawdry TV shows and Hollywood portrayals of uncommitted, bed-hopping sex. Our familiarity with love diminishes its significance and our misuse of the word distorts its power.

But love is at the heart of our understanding of God's great narrative played out across the span of Scripture. "Love" appears over 750 times in the Bible. It is the core of God's story and His very being. It is the essence of His mission. Love is the center of God's two great commands to us—to love God and to love our neighbor.[9] There are many attributes that we can possess, but "the greatest of these is love."[10] *The Message* paraphrases this oft-

---

8   Ellison Research, *Outreach* magazine (September/October 2008)
9   Matthew 22:36–38
10   1 Corinthians 13:13

quoted chapter of 1 Corinthians—"No matter what I say, what I believe, and what I do, I'm bankrupt without love."[11] So when Jesus asks Peter "Do you *love* me?" he is getting to the nub of the matter for him and for us.

John states "Peter was hurt because Jesus asked him a third time, 'Do you love me?' "[12] Peter was not hurt by the recurrent question. In fact, he was likely relieved by Jesus' grace in asking three times in exchange for Peter's three-fold denial. To understand his grief, we must understand the Greek words used by Jesus.

The first time Jesus asks Peter, "Simon son of John, do you truly love me?" he is using the strong Greek word *agape*, which is a selfless, sacrificial love for others.

Peter's responds, "Yes, Lord, you know that I love you"—except that Peter substitutes *phileo*—a deep friendship, for the word *agape*—the unconditional love of God.

Again in verse 16, Jesus asks Peter, "Do you love (*agape*) me?" Peter responds a second time, "Yes, Lord, you know that I love (*phileo*) you." You're my buddy.

Jesus asks the seminal question a third time that ultimately *we* must answer, "Simon son of John, do you love me?" This time, however, Jesus substituted the weaker word *phileo*. He is asking Peter and us, "Do you want to be my buddy, my pal, my friend—OR—are you totally sold out, ready to love me with an abandoned, unconditional, wholehearted love, regardless of the

---

11 1 Corinthians 13:3 (MSG)
12 John 21:17

consequences or price tag?" Is your love for me *agape* or is it *phileo*?

This is *the* question. Are we willing to abandon our busy-ness and the false security that inhibits our intimacy with the Almighty? Are we able to set aside our prejudice and the "narcissism of small differences" that prevents us from loving our neighbors as ourselves? Are we prepared to move from a deep friendship or even a familial love to total devotion to our Creator? Are we sold out to Jesus?

As soon as Peter grasped what Jesus was asking, he was hurt. His faith was being called into question. The fearless follower became more reflective as a result, and never again used the weaker word *phileo* in any of his writings.

Jesus ultimately predicted "the kind of death by which Peter would glorify God."[13] He was crucified upside down for practicing *agape* love of Jesus.

Jesus' last command to Peter, and to us, is to "Follow me."[14] This is what empowered the fearful disciples of John to "come and see" and the fearless followers of Jesus to "go and be." Are we ready to follow? We must first answer for ourselves Jesus' questions of our desire, fear, wholeness, identity, forgiveness, wealth, generosity, and love. Only then are we prepared to practice the fierce faith to which he calls us and for which we will be eternally rewarded in heaven.

---

13 John 21:19
14 John 21:19

It will be thrilling to meet John's disciples, the timid lake-crossers, the beggar of Bethesda, the possessed grave-dweller, the town whore and the well-fed 5,000, Peter, Lester and Jeffrey. It promises to be exhilarating. I can hardly wait. I look forward to meeting you there. Until then, may God richly bless you as you continue to live in His questions.

Chapter Eight

DO YOU TRULY LOVE ME?

READ

the following Scripture:
- 1 Corinthians 13:1–13
- Matthew 22:34–40

REFLECT

on the following questions:

1. Does your service *to* God get in the way of your intimacy *with* God?

2. How do you picture heaven? Who do you most look forward to meeting? With whom do you most look forward to reuniting?

3. Do you practice *agape* or *phileo* love for God?

RESPOND

to the following challenge:

- Assess your time commitments. Do any of your priorities—work, relationships, health, finances—need to be reprioritized so that they do not diminish your devotion to God? Seek to reprioritize your schedule over the next 30 days.

A Word After

The process of getting my beliefs and stories articulately on these pages has been exacting. That alone has taken me four years. But it has been much more difficult to push aside dark thoughts that come at 3 a.m.—the ones that say, "Who do you think you are, writing a book on faith? You're a fraud! You struggle with everything you are writing about in this book!"

It is said we write and speak about that which we long to learn. This has certainly been true for me with these *8 Questions God Can't Answer*. I am challenged daily by discerning God's desire for my life, overcoming my own fears, seeking wholeness, claiming my identity as a Jesus-follower, extending genuine forgiveness, understanding true wealth, practicing real generosity and wholeheartedly loving God. I believe all of this is possible, but it is a full-contact sport!

I echo the father of the son cured by Jesus in Mark's gospel: "I do believe: help my unbelief." Help me overcome my 3 a.m. doubts. Help me faithfully lean into these questions. Help me to truly practice what I write.

I am making it all a matter of daily prayer. Not just any prayer though. I am taking a shot at living the prayer penned by Brennan Manning:

"I surrender my will and my life to you today, without reservation and with humble confidence for you are my loving Father.

Set me free from self-consciousness, from anxiety about yesterday and tomorrow and from the tyranny of the approval and disapproval of others, that I may find joy and delight simply and solely in pleasing you.

Let your plan for my life and the lives of all your children gracefully unfold one day at a time."

Set us free to say yes to Jesus' penetrating questions. Yes to Jesus' provocative stories. Yes to Jesus' perplexing miracles. Help us believe that these are not just His teaching technique, but truly His deep desire for our life.

Help our unbelief.

Acknowledgments

To Carol—my wife, soul mate and best friend since high school, who knows me through and through, and still loves me, for your undying support of this process the last 4 years, and of me for more than 30 years.

To Brett and Josh—our two great sons, for your love, your insightful reading, tough questions and deep source of inspiration for this book.

To our Friday guy's group—Roger, Tom W., Tom L., Mark, Phil, John, Keith, Lee, Apham, Kevin and Dan, and our adopted son, Larry—you all are an inspiration to me, a ready source of authentic life stories and the reason I did not quit on this project when the rejection letters piled up.

To Kent—from a "coincidental" meeting many years ago, you have been an unrelenting source of encouragement, a model of fierce faith and a wise shepherd throughout the writing process.

To Kurt—my friend and inspiring young pastor, whose love of Jesus and authentic faith have kept my own belief plugged in these last 4 years.

To John and Laura—our friends, whose leading question, "How's the book?" and deep interest in Carol and me have fueled my passion for this project and for God's church.

To Tom, Shoe Bob, Elias, Stefan, Nathan, my Ghanaian brothers and sisters, Pastor Jack and his cool ninth graders—all of whose stories inspired me from up close, and Dorothy, Mark, Blair and Sandra—whose stories engaged from afar, for your willingness to be transparent.

To Steve— my friend and breakfast or lunchtime sounding board, for your unceasing prayers for our family, especially in the dark moments.

To Paul—my friend and encourager, who has been willing to lend his critical eye and linguistic brilliance to an emerging manuscript, and whose introduction to Keith resulted in a modern-day miracle12 years later.

To John, Larry and Tim—early adopters in their churches, for your willingness to test how God's questions ignite people's faith and stir their soul.

To Norb and Steve—passionate followers of Jesus and practitioners of pastoral care, for your deep investment in my own faith journey the last 12 years.

And to my mom and dad—for loving me enough to start me down this path of faith as a little boy, and for still praying for me today.

About the Author

John Busacker is President of The Inventure Group, a global leadership-consulting firm, and Founder of Life-Worth, LLC, a life planning creative resource. He is a sought-after speaker and facilitator on self-leadership and personal engagement through executive education programs at Duke Corporate Education, the Wharton School of the University of Pennsylvania and the University of Minnesota Carlson School's Executive Development Center.

His travels have taken him to six continents to work with leading organizations such as Medtronic, CJ Corporation of S. Korea, Ameriprise Financial, Pricewaterhouse Coopers, the Good Samaritan Foundation, Boston Children's Hospital, Calvert Investments, Unum and The Pastoral Leadership Institute. John annually teaches in a variety of emerging faith communities and supports the development needs of leaders in Africa through the Duke Divinity School and PLI-International.

John is the author and architect of Life-Based Financial Planning™, a leading-edge system for aligning finances with life values and personal purpose. As a commentator on life/work issues, John has appeared in the The Wall Street Journal, L.A. Times, Minneapolis Star Tribune Research magazine and Experience Life Magazine.

John is an avid explorer, occasional marathoner and novice cyclist. He and his wife, Carol, live in Minneapolis and have two sons, Brett and Joshua.

We invite you to continue your experience with
8 Questions God Can't Answer
by visiting our website:

8 Questions God Can't Answer ?

www.8questionsbook.com

- To purchase additional copies of *8 Questions God Can't Answer*,
contact one of the following:

www.inventuregroup.com/8questionsbook

www.amazon.com
for single copies and small quantities

www.believerspress.com
or any local bookseller

- For bulk purchases of *8 Questions God Can't Answer*:
www.stl-distribution.com

- To book John to speak to your organization or group,
please contact:

John Busacker
(612) 424-7406
-or-
john@8questionsbook.com